Conflicting Agendas

conflicting
agendas

Personal Morality
in Institutional Settings

D. Don Welch

The Pilgrim Press
Cleveland, Ohio

The Pilgrim Press, Cleveland, Ohio 44115

Library of Congress Cataloging-in-Publication Data
Welch, Don, 1947–
    Conflicting agendas : personal morality in institutional settings / D. Don Welch.
       p. cm.
    Includes bibliographical references and index.
    ISBN 0-8298-1001-3
    1. Professional ethics. 2. Corporate culture.
3. Individualism. 4. Decision-making (Ethics)
5. Organizational behavior—Moral and ethical
aspects. I. Title.
BJ1725.W45 1994
174–dc20   94-6912
              CIP

For Mom and Dad,
who introduced me to institutions
and to morality.

Contents

Acknowledgments

Many people have contributed to this book, knowingly and unknowingly, in the dozen or so years in which it has taken shape. I would like to thank Howard Harrod for introducing me to the thought of H. Richard Niebuhr; Kent Richards for his particularly encouraging words in the early stages of the project; Rick Helms for our extended conversations on these issues; and Richard Brown for his editorial wisdom and advice.

I am especially appreciative of the contributions made by those who read earlier drafts of the manuscript and offered their constructive comments: Dan Cornfield, Joe Hough, Doug Knight, Patricia Jung, John Lachs, Pat Rettew, and Dick Zaner.

I am also thankful to Janis Martin for her word-processing services and to Teresa Lyons-Oten for her assistance in the production of the manuscript.

Finally, I must acknowledge that I cannot find the words to recognize adequately the contributions that Gay Welch has made to my life and work.

Introduction
It's Everybody's Problem

Roger Boisjoly had a problem. He was a senior engineer on the Morton Thiokol project that designed the solid rocket boosters for the space shuttle *Challenger*. The day before the January 28, 1986, scheduled launch of the *Challenger* a cold front had dropped temperatures at the launch site at Cape Canaveral, Florida. Boisjoly and other Morton Thiokol engineers were convinced that the shuttle's O-rings, the rings designed to prevent pressure, heat, and flames from escaping through the boosters' joints, might not be able to seal in such cold weather.

Some of Thiokol's engineers had long been concerned about the O-ring design. In an effort to get management more interested in a seal redesign effort, Boisjoly had written a memo describing the seriousness of the O-ring problem. In the event of a failure of the O-rings to seal, he wrote, "The result would be a catastrophe of the highest order—loss of human life."[1]

The night before the scheduled launch, Boisjoly's problem came to a head. The concern expressed by the engineers led to a teleconference involving representatives and officials from Morton Thiokol and the National Aeronautics and Space Administration (NASA). The Thiokol engineers were given an opportunity to explain why they believed it would be unsafe to fly the next day. Boisjoly argued strenuously against the planned launch and recommended not launching until the ambient temperature had reached at least fifty-three degrees Fahrenheit.

Boisjoly then watched as NASA officials pressured Thiokol to reconsider the engineers' recommendations. Going off-line for five minutes, the Thiokol participants gathered to discuss the situation among themselves. "We have a management decision to make," said the senior Thiokol official in the group, who then instructed the company's vice-president for engineering: "It's time to take off your engineer's cap and put on your manager's cap." As a manager, the vice-president had to be concerned about the reputational and possible financial impact on the company if the launch were delayed. Soon thereafter the teleconference with NASA resumed, and NASA officials were informed of the company's conclusion: although conditions for launching were not desirable, they were acceptable.

At that point, Boisjoly and the other engineers acquiesced. They acquiesced not in the sense that they agreed with the conclusion but that they submitted to the authoritative decision. They did not take their case to higher NASA officials, to superiors at Morton Thiokol, or to the press. The next day the *Challenger* was launched. Shortly after take-off an explosion tore the shuttle apart, killing all of the astronauts on board. The official report of a presidential commission concluded that sufficient information about the O-ring problem existed before the accident to have prompted an indefinite launch delay.

This book will examine the kind of conflict faced by Roger Boisjoly and the way we respond when we encounter such conflicts. While the stakes are rarely as high as they were for Boisjoly, the problem is a common one. The challenges of making personal choices in an institutional context are recurring and complex because we are simultaneously immersed in groups and yet distinct from them. We are a part of institutions that exert enormous pressures on us in molding our conduct, but the conduct they would mold is often not the conduct we would otherwise choose for ourselves.

On the one hand, our decisions and actions are shaped and colored by the institutions with which we associate ourselves. I recall sitting at the corner of a large conference table on a sunny afternoon at an Ivy League university, being told that we participants should resist "government interference." Of course there were problems, but we should be allowed to "handle the problems ourselves." These were "educational matters," into which political pressures and governmental processes should not intrude. The bureaucrats in Washington were just not sensitive to the real problems that would be caused by any solution dictated from the nation's capital.

As the participants in the discussion forged a consensus on these points, I was struck by the irony of the deliberation. I had heard similar conversations as forced desegregation had become a reality. But I was not sitting in a public schoolroom in the South in the 1960s. These people were not parents who were beginning to start a private school to avoid busing, but leaders from thirty of the most prestigious private colleges and universities in the country, twenty years later. The issue was whether a national testing service that administered college entrance exams should be required to publish the answers to its tests after the tests were taken. Several groups were demanding the publication of answers both because mistakes had been discovered in the past and out of a desire to analyze the scoring of the tests for cultural bias. Bills were being written in Congress that would mandate the release of the answers being used to grade the tests.

I imagined that each of the men and women in this conference room had, a decade or more earlier, rejected the kinds of arguments that they were now espousing. I did not attribute the change in the way they viewed this line of reasoning to a radical shift in their personal values since the days they voted for Kennedy, Johnson, and Humphrey. For I also imagined that each of these persons would argue persuasively the opposite side of the debate if he or she worked on the staff of the senator who was sponsoring legislation to disclose answers to the tests. The determinative factor in the "keep the government out" rhetoric appeared to be not a philosophical understanding of the appropriate role of government but rather their own positions within the hierarchies of a set of particular institutions.

This afternoon conference illustrated the pull that group membership exerts on us. We are not simply autonomous individuals reaching our own conclusions and pursuing our own interests. We decide and act both as individuals and as members of larger groups. We play these dual roles in the same instant, and sometimes these roles conflict. These dual roles are not a matter of acting as a group member on one occasion and as my "real self" on another. My "real self" comes out of those groups to which I belong. My perspective on the world, the information that is available to me, and the way I respond to those realities are all influenced by my situation within larger social bodies. Thus in a sense the conflicts we experience are not those between a personal self and a social self, but between different social selves. The pervasiveness of this social dimension and the challenge it presents to traditional ways of thinking has been identified by Amitai Etzioni:

> The neoclassical assumption that the individual is the decision-making unit is changed here to assume that social collectivities (such as ethnic and racial groups, peer groups at work, and neighborhood groups) are the prime decision-making units. Individual decision-making often reflects, to a significant extent, collective attributes and processes. Individual decisions do occur, but largely within the context set by various collectivities.[2]

While our decisions are shaped by institutions, while this intermingling of the personal and corporate dimensions of the self is very real, in most cases problems arise because of the distinctions between these two dimensions. Personal behavior within an organizational setting is a recurring problem because a person rarely experiences complete congruence between personal beliefs and institutional imperatives. Individuals affiliate with larger groups for a variety of reasons. Almost inevitably, however, that affiliation imposes duties and obligations that at times are at odds with personal desires and values—or with the duties and obligations we have incurred in other institutional relationships. Almost inevitably, sooner or later, we find ourselves in a position similar to that faced by Roger Boisjoly.

The challenge, of course, is to find some productive ways of thinking about this interplay between the personal and the corporate. How do the social collectivities identified by Etzioni set the context for individual decisions? If these collectivities are indeed a "legitimate and integral part" of our personal existence,[3] how do we envision individual decisions that are in some ways distinctive from the collective decision?

Professional ethics has considered seriously the problem of personal action in an institutional setting. We can gain some insight into the problem being explored in this book by looking at some of the recent work in that field. But I also want to use this work in professional ethics to make a very important point: *the problem of personal morality in institutional settings is everybody's prob-*

lem. The difficulties that motivate this book are faced by everyone who is a member of a family, a neighborhood, a church or a club— not just a group of self-identified professionals. And we all experience and respond to these dilemmas in fundamentally the same way.

Much of the work in professional ethics in recent years has focused on the distinctiveness of the ethics of the professions. Alan Goldman has described the views of those in the professions who believe that their professional duties must outweigh what would otherwise be morally overriding considerations, that special norms and principles should guide their conduct.[4] We've been told that professionalism embodies a standard of good conduct that goes beyond the norms of morality that ordinarily govern relations among persons.[5] The idea, however, is not that professionals must meet the same moral standards as the rest of us and then go beyond those, but that their distinctive moral standards may conflict with the requirements of "ordinary morality."

Codes of professional ethics are, for Michael Davis, conventions among professionals that are produced when an occupation becomes a profession. "What conscience would tell us to do *absent* a certain convention is not necessarily what conscience would tell us to do *given* that convention." The existence of such professional codes means that professionals are not permitted to engage in the weighing of the kinds of interests and factors that is allowed by ordinary morality.[6] Therefore, they are, to an extent, exempt from judgment based on moral standards outside the particular subcommunity that has its own distinctive moral ethos. The sense that one gets from reading most of the professional ethics literature is that, compared to the world of ordinary ethics, the demands placed on professionals are more compelling, the reasoning required of them is more sophisticated, and the compromises they make are morally superior.

I am convinced that the distinctions are overdrawn and that we all experience and respond to ethical dilemmas in basically the same way. The efforts to identify special concepts of morality for professionals create distracting distinctions that separate out pieces of the moral life that can be better understood as integral parts of a whole. I am not arguing that professionals do not have to respond to particular expectations that make a difference in the moral choices they make. The argument, rather, is that everyone is continually engaged in exactly the same process of moral deliberation.

The following example illustrates this point. Experts on professional ethics usually don't consider truck drivers to be members of the club. Let's consider a truck driver who is headed for El Paso, Texas, in June to deliver a load of furniture. The company for which she works has instructed her to drop off the furniture, then drive empty forty miles to Las Cruces, New Mexico, to pick up a load of onions to take back to Atlanta, if she can, or as close to Atlanta as she can arrange. A day out of El Paso our trucker needs to call ahead to Las Cruces to begin setting up the onion load.

The truck driver has had a long and mutually satisfactory relationship with a truck broker who works out of Las Cruces in the summer. Over the years these two individuals have come to rely on the services each can provide the other, the trucker sometimes helping out the broker by taking a load that really didn't fit her own needs best, the broker sometimes giving the trucker special consideration in arranging loads with shippers. The trucker also knows that the dispatcher for the largest produce shipper in Las Cruces is willing to deal directly with truckers. A call to that dispatcher might produce a better load more quickly and result in an arrangement that would save the trucker the brokerage fee.

So the truck driver has to decide which people to call. She also has to decide what to say when she calls. She does not expect to arrive in Las Cruces until late Saturday afternoon. She knows that none of the shippers want to wait that late to load a truck on Saturday, and they usually don't work on Sunday. She also knows that if she tells them she will be there Saturday morning and gets a commitment for a load on that basis, she will get loaded when she arrives late, even if it takes until midnight. Does she communicate her plans honestly, guaranteeing a two-day layover, or does she attempt to strike a deal based on a commitment she knows she can't keep?

She also knows that the probability of getting exactly what she wants—an 800-bag load with one drop in Atlanta for $1.85 per bag—is fairly low. One-drop loads to Atlanta are easy for brokers and shippers to cover. She can expect that the initial offers will be for loads to places like Dothan, Tallahassee, and Chattanooga, with deliveries to be made at possibly three or four or more different places. While she knows she would accept one of these as a last resort, she doesn't want to give up too easily on more attractive possibilities. How honest should she be in her negotiations in terms of what she would be willing to accept?

Our driver knows that 790 fifty-pound bags of freshly loaded onions are all that she can carry within the legal weight limits of some states she'll be crossing. An 800-bag load is standard, but onions dry out in transit, and she can probably be within legal limits with an 800-bag load by the time she hits the first open scales. A refusal to accept a larger load increases the difficulty of getting a load in a timely fashion. If the route offered is one that makes the probability of detection low enough to be worth the risk to her, should she be willing to accept a load that exceeds legal limits?

In the course of these transactions, this truck driver will be under considerable pressure to (1) violate obligations incurred in a long-standing relationship, (2) make promises she can't keep, (3) be dishonest in negotiations with others, and (4) disobey the law. These seem to be some of the same kinds of moral dilemmas that pose the greatest problems for professionals. Further, while truck drivers may not have a written code of ethics that has been approved by a formal association, they do operate in a world of deeply entrenched mores and practices. To use Davis's term, conventions exist in the world of truckers, brokers, and dispatchers that are recognized by all the participants. The truck driver makes these decisions in response to the expectations embodied in these customs and norms, not as an isolated individual.

The participants in this situation—the brokers, dispatchers, packing shed operators, other truckers—would not be surprised to find our truck driver making promises she could not keep or disobeying the law. The standard of practice in this occupation may well be to act in ways that would be deemed unethical in the abstract or in ordinary circumstances. She may even be expected to act in such ways. My interest at this point is not in exploring whether it is wrong to follow vocational expectations that one be less than fully honest, but in asking whether that matter should be considered differently for professionals than for the rest of us.

Professional standards seem to have been accorded a special significance, simply because they are deemed professional.

Commentators have suggested several features that divide the professions from other pursuits.[7] The question is whether any of these features justify assigning greater moral weight to the norms that exist in those types of professional subcultures. A consideration of four often-identified characteristics of a profession illustrates why I am doubtful that an adequate grounding exists for morally differentiated professional ethical analysis and sheds some light on the way "ordinary" people respond to similar moral dilemmas.

Most lists of features of professions mention that they provide services that are important to society. In recent years, however, we have seen many examples of people starving to death because of a lack of a distribution system. We know that truck drivers provide an important service to society. Airplane mechanics, fire fighters, and farmers, to mention only a few examples, also feel that they provide an important service to society but find themselves on few lists of professionals. We are sometimes told that professionals are committed to some good larger than their own self-interest. But we expect many others also to be committed to a good that transcends their own self-interest: mothers and fathers, United Way volunteers, scout masters, lay religious leaders, soldiers, and police officers, to name a few. Even if service to society does provide a basis for separating the professions from some occupational pursuits, it seems that that feature would argue for less moral insularity, not more. The more crucial a service is to a community, the greater the community's stake is in seeing that the service is rendered in ways that are morally appropriate in light of prevailing societal standards.

Another feature often associated with the professions is the fact that they are granted a degree of autonomy by society, sometimes including a societal-granted monopoly for the services they render. This autonomy usually entails judgment by peers, a certain insulation from lay judgment and control. Rather than providing a grounds for the claimed moral distinctiveness, however, this feature seems to be simply another statement of that distinctiveness.

There is a third feature of the professions that does give a basis for arguing for a certain kind of moral distinctiveness: the nature of professional services requires skills and knowledge not possessed by the population at large. Professions entail extensive training with a significant intellectual component. The problems and moral dilemmas encountered by professionals simply cannot be accurately assessed by lay people.

While the third feature seems on point, it is important that we not claim too much for it. This characteristic of professions may have much to say about *who* engages in moral assessments of professional behavior; it may say very little about *how* those people should make those assessments. Esoteric knowledge and specialized training may limit the number of people who can ably analyze a professional problem. These features, however, do *not* require that those able people analyze that problem using ethical modes of reasoning that are different from those of "ordinary morality."[8]

Rather than seeking discontinuity, I think it is important to identify what a truck driver has in common with doctors and lawyers. In fact, at this point, I want to enlarge the conversation to address the continuities between the ethics of the professionals and those of every other person who plays a distinctive role in our community—that is, all of us. So the discussion includes not only those driving trucks and engaged in other occupations, but also mothers and fathers, participants in political parties and neighborhood organizations, citizens, members of churches and synagogues. Davis is right that the conventions that exist among us affect our moral choices. We face such conventions, however, in every role we play.

The focus of this book is on personal choice in institutional contexts. The terms *institution* and *corporate setting* are used here in their broadest meanings, encompassing virtually all of human existence.[9] Institutions are the patterns that structure our life together, the established ways of shaping and giving meaning to our individual and collective experience. Such institutions include families, civic clubs, ethnic groups, and a host of other social collectivities. All of our decisions are made within the context of various social institutions. Thus the argument in this book assumes and reinforces the continuity between what has been labeled personal and private morality on the one hand, and social or public morality on the other.[10] This rejection of a two-moralities approach to ethics allows us to focus on the common elements of morality that illuminate the decisions we make in social contexts.

In order to advance our understanding of the place of the individual in an institution, we should look at one other feature that is sometimes mentioned as being characteristic of the professions.

Individuals incur certain obligations as they enter into a profession. They pledge to abide by a code of ethics, they covenant with others to uphold the standards of that profession, they agree to act in accordance with professional expectations. This kind of contracting among members of a profession creates limits on the extent to which one can act as an individual agent. Of course, our truck driver may have certain kinds of contractual obligations—for example, with the company for which she works. But is important to look beyond these kinds of formal obligations. Agreements like employment contracts and official codes of ethics are not the only sources for moral decision making. We are also subject to the conventions and expectations of family, friends, and members of nonvocational groups.

The common thread, the source of an "ordinariness" in professional ethics, is that all of us, in all aspects of our lives, are subject to moral claims inherent in the roles we play. This feature of role morality is not, of course, a new insight.[11] But the well-established features of role morality render unremarkable the weaker claims of professional ethics—that professional roles entail obligations. Further, the insights of role morality cast doubt upon the stronger claims, that professional ethics require moral norms and reasoning that are different from those required of ordinary roles. Professional ethics codes do create prima facie duties. So do all of the other relationships that we establish. The difficult questions arise when we find ourselves subject to contradictory prima facie duties.

This book takes this basic insight from professional ethics and expands its relevance into the myriad institutional settings in which we live our lives. The moral dilemmas faced by professionals are fundamentally the same as those we face in all arenas of life. The challenge raised by conflicting expectations in the professions is similar to the challenge raised in everyday life. How do we balance incompatible demands? How do we weigh competing priorities? How do we determine the appropriate answer to the question, "What ought I to do?"

A model that I have found to be particularly helpful in thinking about this issue of personal behavior within an institution is the concept of "agenda." An agenda is a list or outline of items to be discussed or acted upon. Agendas typically provide the planned structure for a meeting, but agendas also establish structure and expectations in other ways. We continually receive commands and opinions, observe events, hear stories, obtain facts and figures, recall histories. In order to assimilate the steady flow of "data," we create organizing principles, typologies, and other interpretive frameworks that enable us to assign meaning and bring understanding to the various problems we encounter. Agendas provide this needed order. They single out particular issues to be given special consideration. They also identify the contexts in which those particular issues are to be addressed and the persons who will be acting on them. This book describes some of the ways in which the concept of the agenda can contribute to our discussion of moral action, and then applies that concept in specific ways to the subject of personal morality in institutional settings.

I do not mean to imply, by focusing on personal responses to institutions, that problems with institutions in our society should be viewed only through such individualistic lenses. There are problems, for example, with the way families and corporations are institutionalized in this culture that call for comprehensive reform, problems that are not addressed by individuals retreating into private life or fleeing from one marriage to another.[12] But some marriages *are* better than others; some people are better suited to one organization than another. This book addresses the responses individuals must continue to make to existing institutions, even as broader efforts at revitalization and reform continue.

Chapter 1 provides a basic description of the notion of the agenda, both in its most common usage as an instrument for formal meetings and in its expanded sense of a device that brings form and structure to various aspects of human activity. In Chapter 2, I have employed the concept of following agendas as a metaphor for human moral action. An analysis of human behavior in terms of agendas is compatible with and contributes to an understanding of a moral theory that stresses responsibility in our actions, in contrast to the traditional models that describe our obligations in terms of obeying rules or striving for goals. The discussion of this theory of moral responsibility, which grows out of the work of H. Richard Niebuhr, provides grounds for assessing the contribution that the idea of the agenda can make to our consideration of particular ethical problems.

The third chapter moves our attention from the general topic of human action to a particular arena of human activity: the social institution. As explained previously, institutions are understood to be not only formal organizations but all of the well-established and structured patterns of relationships that are a fundamental part of our culture. An analysis of the ways persons are located within such institutions leads into an analysis of the obligations that exist in those settings. This chapter takes up the question, "Who sets your agenda?" by looking at the interplay between an individual, other persons, and institutions, in the creation of the lists of things to be done that form our agendas for action.

A typology of personal responses to institutional agendas is developed in part 2. As pure types, these models are artificial. They represent possible responses to the problem of conflicting agendas, whereas real-life responses will often be composed of more than one of these approaches. Indeed, examples presented in these chapters to illustrate one of these types of responses at times embody elements of another type as well.

As Robert Merton pointed out in developing his typology of individual adaptive behavior, categories such as these types refer to types of response to specific situations, not to types of personalities.[13] No person patterns her life in complete conformity to one of these models. In fact, the choice of a response in relation to one institutional agenda can dictate a different response to another agenda. For example, a manager's decision to accept and conform to a corporation's agenda that he work long hours and travel constantly means that that manager will not be accepting and conforming to a family's agenda that he spend the time needed to nurture and care for three young children. This example demonstrates again my argument that the conflict in agendas we encounter is not simply between personal and institutional agendas, but also is a matter of conflicts among a variety of institutional agendas.

While no one chooses any one of these model responses as a consistent guide for action, this examination should help us understand the range of available options by analyzing the features of each and looking at some of the reasons those options have been chosen by others. The purpose of this exercise is not to dictate which responses to make, but to help the reader understand what is going on when responses are chosen.

What types of options are available to individuals faced with conflicting personal and institutional standards? The extreme options would be either wholeheartedly to accept or reject the institution's agenda. A middle-of-the-road approach would be to divide one's life, following the institution's agenda at specified times or for particular functions while reserving other times and tasks for adherence to a personal agenda. Yet another approach would be to seek to alter one agenda or the other in an effort to eliminate the conflict or at least reduce it to a tolerable level. Finally, persons facing this dilemma could try to work out some compromise in their conduct that accommodates primary features of both agenda.

In capsule form, the types discussed in part 2 are described as follows: The *hermit* responds to the conflict between personal and institutional agendas by rejecting the group's agenda and removing herself from the institutional setting. The *institutionalized person* submerges his values into the group's, automatically taking on the institutional agenda as his own. The *split personality* finds value in both agendas and compartmentalizes her life into personal and institutional realms, giving priority to each agenda in the respective settings. The *reformer* seeks to resolve the agenda conflict by reforming the institutional agenda into one that is more compatible with his own. The *accommodator* searches for compromise, attempting to chart a course that is responsive to core elements in both agendas without eliminating the tension between them. Each of the accommodating strategies takes account of one's personal agenda, yet restricts its effect, when determining actions to be taken. The *convert* compares the personal and institutional values in conflict and decides to embrace the values of the group.

In order to provide a continuing basis for comparison among these types of responses, a single case will be used throughout these chapters to illustrate the practical significance of each model. The case involves a young man who, as part of his personal agenda, has developed an expectation that he will not discriminate against other persons because of their race or gender. This young man, we will call him "John," has embraced religious teachings and political philosophies that stress the dignity owed to each individual. Thus, one of his "things to do" is to treat people fairly—for him this means treating them without racial- or gender-related prejudice. He expects to avoid disadvantaging others and, in some circumstances, even to act positively in ways that affirm this view of equality.

John is a member of a private country club. Membership in

this club has been a tradition in his family. The club membership provides a variety of professional, social, and recreational opportunities to him and his family that are not available elsewhere in the community. John's closest friends and associates belong to the club, and its activities are the focus of their social life. The club does not have formal rules forbidding members of minority groups from joining, but only whites are members. The process of approving the few new members that are selected each year from the many aspiring applicants seems to make any deviation from the all-white membership very unlikely. In fact, it appears to be an expectation of the club that only whites will be approved for membership.

John joined the club before his commitment to equal treatment was as fully developed as it is now. John has also recently come to see that the reality of the membership selection process changes the meaning that the absence of official discriminatory policies might have. How does John respond to this situation? The chapters in part 2 describe the options among which he can choose and explore the reasons why a person might choose one strategy over another.

The value of the typology described here does not depend on this particular kind of example. The hypothetical example could just as easily have been about Maria, the regional vice-president of a large petrochemical company. She considers herself to be an environmentalist. Indeed, one factor that influenced her decision to accept employment with this company was its excellent reputation as an environmentally progressive manufacturer. Maria discovers an internal company report, one that was "buried" by her predecessor, that suggests that one of the older, larger plants in her region may be illegally dumping waste on company land. The report was ignored because of its tentative conclusion that the plant could not be brought into compliance with new environmental standards in a cost-effective way. If the choice were to comply or close, the choice would probably be to close. The more attractive financial alternative was found to be to continue current practices, viewing the potential government fines as an acceptable cost of doing business.

Maria thus faces a conflict between her personal agenda— involving not only her environmental commitment but also her conviction that no person or company should be above the law—

and institutional expectations. These expectations include those of stockholders and board members that she will act to promote company profits. Continued operation with a willingness to pay prospective fines seems to be the profit-maximizing option. She also faces the expectations of loyal company employees, as well as those of residents of the small community that would be devastated by a plant closing, that their well-being will be taken into account in corporate decision making.

How should Maria respond to this set of circumstances? What is the appropriate resolution of this value conflict? You may prefer to trace this example, or one of your own making, as you explore the meanings of the types of responses described in part 2.

Part 3 addresses the choice that we all must make. Each of us must choose our agenda or agendas; each of us must identify the claims we will accept as authoritative for us and the ways we will respond to the competing obligations that confront us. The attempt in this final section is not to specify the content of a universal agenda, but to shed some light on the process of adjudicating the conflicting claims upon us.

By using the notion of agenda as a guiding metaphor for reflecting on morality, the discussion in this book avoids the dichotomies that are often employed to separate out parts of our moral life, such as public/private, personal/social, and professional/unprofessional. Further this metaphor embraces all of the moral expectations that evoke our response. Thus, the interminable debate between teleologists and deontologists is also avoided. Those divisive and compartmentalizing concepts are replaced by a holistic approach to our moral life that helps make sense of the value conflicts we continually encounter as we make our way in the institutions that constitute the fields for moral decision making.

Part I

Understanding
Personal Morality

1

Agendas

An agenda[1] is, quite simply, a list of things to be done. While the term is perhaps most often used with reference to a plan or list of items to be discussed or acted upon at a meeting, common usage incorporates a broader meaning for the word. There are clearly "things to be done" in all aspects of our lives, and thus we are quite comfortable speaking of agendas outside the conference room. With apparent mutual understanding, we regularly speak of a variety of agendas (common and hidden, national and personal, unfinished, formal, or full) in relation to a host of personal and social activities. An examination of what agendas are and how they function can give us a fuller understanding of human behavior—particularly in the context of a complex social institution.

The Formal Meeting Agenda

On the face of it, a formal meeting agenda is a fairly simple matter. It conveys information about the structure of a meeting: time, place, persons involved, topics to be addressed, perhaps suggestions about background material or preparatory work. The expressed purpose of this type of agenda is to promote an efficient use of time and ensure that important items are covered adequately. At a more basic level, however, an agenda establishes common expectations about future activity and provides a structure that is used to judge the appropriateness of individuals' behavior.

Agendas can provide an agreed-upon basis for people to get together and work cooperatively. This often occurs informally among a group of people who have interacted over a long period of time. In such a situation, common goals are understood and methods of working are mutually respected. A more formal agenda spells out specifically the details of the work to be done and how it is to be accomplished. This kind of public agenda lets us know what to expect.

Initially, an agenda offers a basis for deciding whether or not to participate in a meeting. Persons are informed that there is a "full agenda," meaning that the meeting is worthwhile and one's presence is justified. People see that a meeting is covering important matters and thus they choose to attend. Or that it is covering matters that are trivial or of little interest to the reader of the agenda who decides not to attend. The importance of a meeting can also be signaled by the people who are not in attendance but who are directly interested in the meeting, as indicated by their receipt of copies of the agenda.

An agenda gives structure to the meeting once the participants have gathered: determining the subject matter, setting boundaries for discussion, even directing the actions to be taken. By focusing the awareness of the group on a particular topic, time and energy are used economically. The items that are deemed important (whether chosen by the group or by a single person convening the meeting) are more likely to be addressed appropriately within a structured meeting.

There are types of agendas that run counter to the purposes of this public, formal meeting agenda. The "hidden agenda" is not intended to establish common expectations. Rather than creating a common basis for working together, its purpose is the manipulation of a group to reach goals without a common effort, or at least without group awareness of common effort. Such a tactic is relied upon when a common basis for achieving an end is lacking, or even when the chosen end stands in opposition to the shared interests or perspectives of group members. The "personal agenda" is another variation from the common agenda. Individuals pursue personal agendas when they are convinced of the validity of their own opinions or chosen course of action, often with the hope of gaining group approval or at least group acquiescence.

Hidden or personal agendas are usually viewed unfavorably by those attending a meeting. The public agenda establishes group expectations, one of those being that it will bring structure to that meeting and that that structure will be used to evaluate the behavior of individuals. An item on the agenda has legitimacy as a topic of concern and action. When someone departs from the agenda, there are expressions of boredom, a feeling that time is being wasted, a fear that any limits on the boundaries of the discussion will be lost. An unscheduled topic is clearly viewed as unimportant (or else it would have been on the agenda) or not appropriate at this time (it can be put on the agenda for a later meeting). The pursuit of hidden agendas can be quite dysfunctional for the institution.[2]

People ask to be placed on the agenda so that whatever they have to say can be taken seriously. Formal agendas often include such topics as "miscellaneous" or "other business" to legitimize additional comments that someone might wish to make. Agendas can be changed. Altering an agenda during the course of a meeting usually obligates those presiding to offer a justification when asking the consent of the group to make the change. The success of meetings is judged by the agenda. "That covers everything on the agenda" means that the meeting can end, we have done our duty—although it says nothing about how the various agenda items were handled. I was in one meeting which ended with the declaration that the agenda had been covered, and all seven agenda items had been carried over for further discussion at the next meeting!

If a person is at a meeting without a copy of the agenda, he or she is inhibited from participating. The fear always exists that if one speaks up, the response will be, "We'll take that up under item number six." Such a response implies personal incompetence on the part of the offender and could taint the substance of whatever that person wishes to say—if he speaks at all—when the group does address item number six. Indeed, using agendas in such a fashion is one of the "control techniques" that has been suggested for use by administrators: "Establish meeting agenda and time slots, and publish and distribute the agenda well in advance of the next meeting. Do not allow items not on the agenda to be discussed. Speakers on the agenda items should be diplomatically cut off at the end of the time scheduled."[3]

If meetings can be awkward when someone departs from the agenda, they can be disastrous in the absence of an agenda. Without the sense of direction that comes from an agenda (whether formal or informal), a meeting becomes a purposeless gathering of warm bodies. If the convener of a meeting fails to attend and no agenda has been planned in advance, there is a good chance the assembled people will dismiss themselves. I recall attending a meeting where this happened, even though the working relationships of the people gathered were such that a variety of common interests could have been discussed and a number of problems resolved through their combined efforts. But without a commonly agreed upon set of expectations the meeting simply did not take place.

The need for an agenda is especially pronounced if the participants have not already established an informal network of relationships or activities. In the late 1960s I participated in two different efforts to bring together students from predominantly black campuses and predominantly white campuses. I learned the lesson: when dealing with people from different subcultures, developing formal common expectations is of the utmost importance. The question "Why are we here?" consumed entire meetings and was never really answered. Both projects ended in failure because they lacked defined purposes. There were no shared agendas.

Meetings without agendas of some sort are candidates for chaos. Some sense of the people, the issues, and the context that control the meeting is necessary before conversations can lead to meaningful communication and finally to a shared decision-making process. While agendas can emerge after a group has assembled, formal meeting agendas have become routinely used tools in the service of efficiency and effective decision making. In summarizing the function of an agenda, we could say that it tells us (1) who counts, (2) what matters, and (3) the context (the time and place) within which we will respond to the expectations that those people (the ones who count) have developed on those issues (the ones that matter).

When an agenda for a meeting is distributed, a community of agents is defined, the people *who count* are identified. A particular person or group of persons writes the agenda; other people receive the document. Still other persons can become parties to the agenda—as bystanders who have a stake or an interest in the items to be acted upon and have been informed formally of the upcoming proceeding.

The expectations that are contained in this list of things to be done are tied up in an understanding of who counts. We do not respond to any set of agenda items in a vacuum. Our reaction to an agenda, indeed our very understanding of what that agenda is, is shaped by the community of persons that are associated with it. Our decisions are made as we listen to people speaking to us and as we anticipate what will be said in response to our decisions. When we establish who counts, when we choose which voices to listen to and whose future opinions we will take into account as we ponder our choices, we go a long way toward making our substantive decisions.

In addition to telling us who counts, an agenda tells us *what matters*. Some items are included on an agenda; others are left off. We respond not only to people who count, but to particular topics. Specific subjects are identified as important for this particular meeting. Other subjects are not necessarily unimportant, but they are deemed less relevant in this context. An agenda is made up of the subjects to which we are paying serious attention, thus narrowing the potentially boundless list of items to a shorter list that can provide a manageable focus of attention.[4]

The definition of the *context* for decision making is a third function served by a meeting agenda. A time and place for the meeting are identified. A factor that textures the consideration of any issue is the location in which conversations take place. An agenda, however, communicates more about the context than simply the place. The institution, or the office or division within an institution, is indicated as the "host" for the meeting. This sponsorship often figures in the characterization of the context for decision. As a context is identified in these various ways, certain values and concerns become more legitimate as bases for discussion about the issues at hand.

An agenda provides the legitimating structure for a meeting. It defines the participants, the circumstances, and the subject matter to be considered. It develops common expectations for discussion and action and creates parameters within which personal responses should fall. If an agenda does not exist prior to the gathering of a group of people, one must be developed (formally or informally, explicitly or implicitly) as a precondition for group action.

Agendas beyond the Conference Room

The way agendas, as "things to be done," bring form and structure to our lives ranges far beyond conference rooms and formal printed announcement of meetings. The ordering function of agendas is present in all forms of human activity, and thus the concept of the agenda is helpful in analyzing types of human behavior other than business meetings. In a variety of contexts, agendas create expectations, establish grounds on which to judge human action, and in some ways even define reality.

We get some indication of how we rely on the expectations of established agendas in our lives when we encounter unanticipated changes. People often become troubled or upset by a change in plans not because the new idea is not as good as the old one but because it is not what was expected. We latch on to certain agendas and find something disturbing about a development that suddenly alters those agendas.

The functioning of agendas can be observed on all levels: from the most elemental aspects of face-to-face interpersonal relations to the actions of nation-states. At the most intimate end of the this spectrum, consider the interaction of two people who encounter one another and begin to engage in conversation. Each person selects certain items to present. Out of an almost boundless personal history, some experience, some feeling, some fact is chosen to be communicated to the other person. That choice is drawn from that person's list of topics that are considered appropriate to be discussed in that setting.

Quite often, the second party will have a different subject on his or her mind. If the conversation is more than a perfunctory exchange, a give-and-take will follow in which these people select the terrain, identifying categories to be used, defining the reality of that conversation in the face of competing possibilities. They will have forged a common agenda for that encounter. (The setting of formal meeting agendas can follow a similar pattern as a tentative agenda is distributed "to test the water" before a final agenda is drafted.)

A shared agenda does not always result from the coming together of two or more persons. In those cases we speak of people talking past each other. An example that comes to mind is an encounter my wife and I had with a salesperson. At the start of our conversation, we were unaware that his agenda was to convince us to sell his product in our spare time. He began by asking us what we would do if we had more money, suggesting extravagant trips and luxurious automobiles as possibilities. Our response was that if we had more money we would work less. This response was a clear indication that we brought a different agenda to the conversation than the one he had in mind for us. The more disparate two people's worldviews are, the more difficulty they will have in establishing common expectations.

Deborah Tannen highlights the importance of shared expectations in conversations in *You Just Don't Understand.* She writes of framing a conversation, much as a frame for a picture provides a context for the images in the picture. She argues that most meaning in conversation is filled in by the person listening, that how one interprets someone else's words depends on the hearer's own focus and concerns. Thus, our reactions to what others say are often sparked by how we feel we are being "framed"[5]— that is, how we expect them to treat us. Attempts to communicate are often confounded and misunderstandings often result when conversations don't proceed with similar frames that are operative for all of the parties in the conversation. Meaningful communication depends on the type of structure provided by agendas.

On a larger scale, the same three elements of who counts, what matters, and the context in which one responds to both also appear at organizational levels such as governmental institutions. A formal governmental agenda has been defined by Roger Cobb and Charles Elder as "that set of items explicitly up for the active and serious consideration of authoritative decision-makers." The things that matter are those items targeted for active and serious consideration, as distinguished from "pseudo-agenda items" that may be put on some list with no intention of meaningful engagement. "In giving an issue formal agenda status, government conveys important messages about who and what are socially important, about what is or is not problematic, and about what does and does not fall within the legitimate purview of government."[6] Commenting on the shaping of a governmental agenda, one group of observers has identified the three basic elements as problems, politics, and participants.[7] In this scheme the participants, the visible actors, tell us who counts. Problems are those conditions that are identified as issues to be addressed, that is, the things that matter. For the government the political process constitutes the circumstances in which the participants act on the issues that have been identified.

Each group to which we belong has certain expectations of us. Each institution has its agenda,[8] and persons associated with a

particular institution feel the presumption, the pressure, that they
will adhere to that particular agenda. As we will see, individuals
respond to these presumptions in many different ways. Individuals
responses are affected by the expectations people have of themselves—their personal agendas.

The Shape of Personal Agendas

Is there such a thing as a personal agenda? We are social
creatures; our knowledge and our values have come to us in social
contexts, through institutions. Can we identify and choose to follow a personal agenda, or are we, in fact, simply choosing among
competing institutional agendas? It is true that the social world
exists prior to any individual. The image of an independent, wholly
autonomous self making moral choices simply does not match our
experience. But while human beings are social products, the social
world is also a human product.[9] The relationship is a dialectical one
in which persons both shape and are shaped by the social institutions that constitute their world.

The kernel of the idea that individuals create their environment (as well as being created by it) is a view of the self that
encompasses both a social "me" and a creative "I."[10] The "I" is the
aspect of the self that responds to social contexts in a self-conscious way. It is a response to community attitudes that interprets
them—thus changing them, insofar as they have meaning for the
individual—and that issues in a novel response. Uncertainty *does*
accompany a person's response to social expectations, and we *do*
make choices in a way that distinguishes a core of the self from the
social being that automatically reacts to external stimuli.

When we choose among competing institutional expectations, we make our choices using some standards, some criteria,
some set of values. In essence we develop some notion of what we
expect of ourselves—our personal agenda. This agenda is shaped
by our encounter with institutional agendas, but we can come to
own it in a real sense. It is comprised of the expectations that we
have embraced—those that strike us as less external, less coercive,
as more consistent with our sense of who we are and what we want
to affirm for ourselves.

According to traditional role theory, relationships are essentially interactions among persons based on shared expectations.

However, we have perceptions of ourselves and our behavior from our own personal point of view—apart from role expectations. Further, we can expect incongruity between "self" and "role," between "I" and "me," an incongruity which yields conflicting expectations.[11] We redefine our personal agendas and fashion our responses to institutional agendas as we resolve new conflicts and make new choices.

Personal agendas have many of the same components that are found in the formal meeting agenda. In particular, personal agendas identify (1) who counts, (2) what matters, and (3) the context in which we respond to the expectations of the people who count on the issues that matter.

In all areas of our lives, agendas identify the persons who make up the reference group for our deliberations and actions as we answer questions about what we ought to do. Sometimes these people are those with whom we speak directly, asking their advice, seeking their opinions, bouncing our ideas off them. In other cases, the people who count are more remote from the actual point of decision. These may be peers in our profession, family members who will view our actions from afar, other residents in our community, or superiors in particular groups to which we belong. The people who count are not only those whose advice we seek but those whose judgments we anticipate as we consider our choices.

Our life agendas, like conference room agendas, also identify what matters. Some issues are presented to us as more important than others. Some concerns are pressed forward as more urgently in need of a response from each of us as an individual. In our daily lives we encounter an almost endless list of causes, projects, problems, and aspirations. As we select from these lists, we determine which issues we will address and which we will not.

Personal agendas also identify a context for decision making. These agendas supply a basis for judging which concerns are appropriate, which responses are fitting, which courses of action are legitimate. They do not simply present identifiable questions for us to answer in an identifiable community of persons. These agendas also lay the groundwork for answering these questions through reference to basic norms and principles that will guide our responses to the world around us.

To a large extent, the process of growing up is a process of developing our personal agendas. Certain aspects of our life agenda began at birth with societal expectations that were established because of our gender, race, social class, and family history. As we become moral agents, as we are able to make our own choices among competing alternatives, we embrace certain agendas as our own. We determine those people who will count in our deliberations. We choose the issues with which we will wrestle. We develop a list of fundamental values and beliefs that will provide basic reference points for us as we continually ask the question, "What should I do?"

A personal agenda, of course, is never a matter that is finally settled. We continue to adjust our agendas as our life's circumstances change, as we encounter new people or are presented with new information or are urged to adopt new causes. The proverbial midlife crisis is an almost inevitable occasion for reevaluating one's agenda, a reevaluation that typically occurs when we discover that we have moved from surveying a broad plain to following a rutted road. The passages described in Gail Sheehy's book[12] are essentially the most prominent points in our continual process of agenda reaffirmation or revision.

The specific concern of this book is to look at what happens when that personal agenda, the agenda that we have embraced as our own, has to share our lives with a corporate agenda—be it the agenda of our company, our church or synagogue, our political party, or any other social institution in which we have membership. Before turning to a discussion of the corporate agenda, however, we will focus more fully on the relation of the concept of the agenda to a particular understanding of moral responsibility.

2

Agendas and Ethical Reflection

We all have our list, or more accurately, lists of things to be done. We enter each situation with our various agendas and respond to those situations accordingly. Most often our responses come easily, without thought. We almost automatically select the appropriate action, playing the role called for by the circumstances at hand. We operate on the basis of agendas that have long since been internalized. We proceed through our everyday routine world without serious reflection upon why we do each of the things we do.

We periodically come upon a situation, however, in which our response does not come immediately. We encounter a set of circumstances that causes us to pause, to consider options or review how fitting the automatic response really is. We are forced to stop and ask the normative question, "What ought I to do?" This kind of reflection is required only when conflict occurs, when an agenda or an item on an agenda is challenged or contested by another item or agenda, or when circumstances change or are so ambiguous that the assumed—or even intentionally chosen— agenda may no longer fit.

For example, we do not normally reflect on breathing. This continuation of a basic life-sustaining activity is an action we take for granted. We do not regularly make conscious decisions about breathing; we are not called upon to reflect ethically about what we should do about breathing. The circumstances are different, however, for some persons who are terminally ill and are sustained by artificial resuscitation devices. Other considerations challenge the taken-for-granted status as the activity is viewed in a

new light. The normative question is then asked in a way that
demands ethical reflection.

Similarly, choosing a seat as we board a bus does not usually evoke thoughts about morality. In most cases we drop our
change in the collection box and move on to an empty seat without
much more thought than considering whether there is an acquain-
tance with whom we wish to sit or an empty seat into which to
deposit our briefcase or shopping bag. For Rosa Parks and Martin
Luther King, Jr., however, the act of choosing a seat on a bus was
full of moral implications. Only when taken-for-granted actions are
challenged in this way does ethical reflection occur. Thus a central
problem for ethics is conflict between loyalties, values, or agendas.

An Ethics of Responsibility

When deciding how we should act, we must have some
way of identifying and sorting through the conflicting elements in
a given set of circumstances. We need some way to analyze the
situation at hand and make some decisions about an appropriate
response. The more complex the setting, the greater the need.
Therefore, I will lay the groundwork for an exploration of the
problem of personal behavior in an institutional setting by first
briefly describing a model of human action.

The view of human action that I have developed is heavily
indebted to the writings of moral philosopher and theologian H.
Richard Niebuhr, particularly to his work in *The Responsible Self*.[1]
In that book, Niebuhr presents his understanding of human action
in the context of two classical images of human morality: the person-as-maker and the person-as-citizen. He then develops his own
alternative of thinking of persons primarily as responders.

The image of the person-as-maker presents human beings
as persons concerned with creating desired ends. Human action is
based upon and judged by the consequences that an act produces.
The appeal is to the comparative amount of good produced or to
the comparative balance of good over evil produced. For example,
a decision to use extraordinary medical procedures on a patient
might be judged to be right if the patient lives. A decision to jump
into a river to rescue a drowning swimmer could be evaluated as a
good one if both swimmer and rescuer reach shore safely. Questions of morality are largely questions of results; individuals are

seen as motivated by achieving goals or creating products. Similarly, ethical reflection upon whether a particular act is right or wrong centers on an analysis of the consequences of that act. An act is right if and only if it produces or is intended to produce at least as great a balance of good over evil as any available alternative. The dictum that "the ends justify the means" expresses this perspective on human morality.

Following this teleological approach humans are viewed as makers, as artisans who construct things according to an idea and for the sake of an *end,* a product or result, by which an act is judged to be good or bad, right or wrong. We all know what it is to act with a purpose, with a future state of affairs in mind. And we all know how important it is to inquire into the effectiveness of the steps taken moment by moment in this movement toward the desired goal. In many affairs of life we employ this practical means-and-ends reasoning. We go to work in order to make money to purchase life's necessities; we take medication to rid our bodies of infection; we canvas door-to-door to promote a "correct" election result. Many moral theories and moral exhortations presuppose the future-directed, purposive character of human action and differ among themselves only in the ends that should be pursued—for example, happiness, wisdom, power, self-actualization, beauty, freedom, peace. But each of these theories conforms to an image of the person-as-maker, the person as technician or artist or artisan.

The person-as-citizen, on the other hand, lives under the law. There are considerations other than consequences that can make an action right or wrong. Morality is not a matter of producing the right results, but of adhering to principles which speak to features of acts themselves rather than their results. Obedience is the major theme. In this view, we are in control of neither the material with which we can build, nor of all of the results of our actions. Thus, we are to be concerned with the processes of living, and value is found in obeying correct—often reasonable—rules or laws.

We live in the midst of mores, of commandments and rules, thou-shalts and thou-shalt-nots, of directions and permissions. Our life must take account of the rules, of the law, of approvals and disapprovals, of social, legal, and religious sanctions. Thus, the moral question in this deontological scheme is not, "What end shall I pursue?" but, "What rule should I follow?"; not,

"What shall I strive for?" but, "What should I *obey*?" The dominant image is one of a citizen obeying those rules and laws that are deemed to be valid. We come into being under the rules of family, community, and nation, subject to the regulation of our actions by others. Against these rules we can and do rebel, yet we find it necessary—morally necessary—to consent to some laws and to give ourselves rules, or to administer our lives in accordance with some discipline.

An alternative posed by Niebuhr to these two approaches is the image of the person-as-responder. According to this image, our actions are viewed neither as attempts to attain ideal goals nor to obey laws, but are basically understood as responses. This understanding of human action is rooted in the shared experience of persons being engaged in dialogue—answering questions, replying to orders, meeting challenges—of persons acting in response to actions upon themselves. Value is found in neither goal achievement nor in obeying laws, but in "fitting action," that is, responses that are appropriate in relation to the context in which one acts. When a person acts appropriately in this sense, that person is acting responsibly. One's duty, rather than producing right consequences or adhering to correct rules, is to be responsible.

Carol Gilligan has described this meaning of responsibility as acting responsively in relationships.[2] Writing about the conflicts of loyalty that we all face, she points out that the self exists in relationship to others and the reference for our moral judgments is that relationship. This morality of response emphasizes our situatedness, our interdependence, our connectedness with others as distinct from moralities that view individuals as principally independent and separate, moralities that stress neutral rules and principles.

The advantage of the responsibility model over the other two models is that it more accurately reflects the nature of human interaction. The images of the person-as-maker and the person-as-citizen both point to aspects of moral action. But both approaches represent only partial truths, oversimplifying the very complex process through which we convert beliefs into deeds.

William Frankena's *Ethics* has probably been used more than any other book to introduce students and others to ethics. Frankena shows his own dissatisfaction with the either/or choice of teleology and deontology by proposing his own theory of obligation which he calls a "mixed deontological theory."[3] His effort to develop an approach that takes into account both the pursuit of certain ends (maximizing the balance of good over evil in the world) and adherence to certain deontological principles (justice; perhaps keeping promises) supports his conclusion that neither approach is adequate on its own. Obeying rules and pursuing ends are only two of many human modes of responding to the world. The concept of response, however, embraces all interactions of the self with other selves and with our environment.

The image conjured up by the notion of persons as makers or citizens is that of a free-standing, autonomous individual looking at some external artifacts and making choices about which goal to pursue or which rule to follow—much as a customer moves down a cafeteria line making choices. Human choice, however, is a much more interactive phenomenon as decisions emerge from involvement in various communities. This choosing incorporates considerations of past and future that are not merely elements to be manipulated by the decision-maker but which themselves shape who the decider is and how she relates to the world. The image of the person-as-responder moves us beyond the misplaced emphasis on autonomy of the other two approaches.

It is clear how the first two models address the ethical question, "What should I do?" If we view persons as makers, we identify the goals that should be achieved or the results that should be produced and then evaluate decisions and actions by how well they lead to the chosen ends. If human beings are understood primarily as citizens, then the moral task is to discover the right laws and rules to be obeyed and judge how closely they are followed. It is not so clear how we are to act responsively, how we are to make moral judgments about the appropriateness of an act in a certain context.

Agendas and Decision Making

We can clarify this concern by drawing connections between the character of a response ethics and the function of agendas described in chapter 1. Indeed, it may be helpful to organize the elements of an ethics of response in terms of the primary factors addressed by agendas: who counts, what matters, and the context in which we respond to the expectations of the persons who count on the issues that matter. If this characterization of the person-as-responder works, then we can appropriate the familiar image of following agendas to enhance our understanding of this approach to ethical decision making.

Who counts? We choose our moral responses with other people in mind: their teachings, their approvals or disapprovals, their abilities to reward or to impose punishment, their continuing associations with us. One aspect of recognizing who counts is captured in Niebuhr's use of the concept of anticipation: we act in anticipation of responses to our responses. We make our decisions knowing that our deeds will produce other responses in reaction to them; we anticipate answers to our answers. Our actions are like statements in continuing conversations, and we seek to make statements that not only fit with the previous statements to which they are replies, but also in anticipation of responses to our statements.

We cannot, of course, be equally concerned about the potential responses of everyone else. Some people count more than others. We place more value on, or at least feel that we should take into account more fully, the anticipated reaction of particular individuals or particular communities. A parallel can be drawn between this element of moral action and the concept from literary theory of a "textual community."[4] The notion is that every text is addressed to certain groups—the implied readers. The sense of community established by an author's thinking about who is included in that group is essential to understanding a text. In the same way, all of our moral acts are addressed to certain communities. Just as texts are influenced by the persons an author considers to be the textual community, so moral decisions are shaped by the persons an actor has in mind as a moral community. These moral decisions can be understood only when that particular community is identified and its relationship to the actor is taken into account.

Another aspect of the element of who counts is the fact that our responses are formed in the midst of communities to which we belong—a reality that also influences answers to the other questions of what matters and the context in which we act. When we respond, we do so as a member of continuing communities. We do not act as beings in isolation, but as individuals who affect and who are affected by other persons. All of our responses are made in light of our relations to others—past, present and future. A key ingredient in answering the question, "What ought I to do?" is the identification of a community in which and to which that person exercises responsibility. Niebuhr captures this element of morality in his notion of "social solidarity."[5]

We can easily imagine situations in which our answer to "What ought I to do?" would vary depending on which group we identified as the appropriate community within which we were acting. For example, an advertising executive will make different decisions depending on whether her primary reference group is a body of peers whose watchword is *caveat emptor* or the parents who taught her to always tell the truth, the whole truth, and nothing but the truth. Therefore, in the same way that an agenda identifies who counts in a formal meeting, the way we fashion our responses identifies who counts in our moral reckoning.[6]

What matters? The response model of ethics characterizes our actions as responses to actions upon us. However, every day countless actions occur that affect us and our world. Before we can make any considered response to the virtually infinite candidates for attention, we have to make some sense of the activities and causes that come our way and decide what really matters to us.

The first step in this process is figuring out what is going on, a step that entails the element Niebuhr identified as interpretation. We identify and analyze events so that they come to us not as brute actions, but as having meaning. We interpret the things that force themselves upon us as parts of wholes, as related to and symbolic of larger meanings. Interpretation is a matter of setting forth meaning, of understanding in a particular way. We are continuously attempting to understand and give meaning to persons, events, and structures that impinge upon our lives. We respond as we interpret the meaning of the actions we encounter, and as we interpret these realities we lay the groundwork for the responses we will make. Our efforts to be responsible are attempts to answer the question, "What should I do?" by raising as the prior question, "What is going on?" or "What is being done to me?" In contrast, in the person-as-maker model the prior question is, "What is my end?" and the person-as-citizen model first asks, "What is my ultimate law?"

Our interpretation of what is going on is affected fundamentally by our perceptions of what matters. My understanding of the events and actions to which I am responding is shaped by the causes, values, goals, beliefs, relationships, and principles that are important to me. In significant ways our agendas serve as interpretive lenses through which we view the world. Just as an agenda raises up for special attention specific topics, so our own personal sense of what matters focuses our powers of discernment and moral energy on certain events while virtually ignoring others. The partial truth of the person-as-maker model is that we each have identified certain goals to pursue, certain ends to achieve. In these goals and ends we have named some things that matter to us. Similarly, the person-as-citizen model rightly construes some of the things that matter to us to be rules or laws which we think are worthy of obedience. But to reduce the things that matter to either a list of desired consequences or a code of rules is inadequate—both to the richness of human life and the complexity of moral decision making. There are also persons to whom we will be loyal, commitments in relationship that we will honor, causes we will support, personal identities we will affirm, affective impulses to which we will yield. As our personal agenda incorporates the sum total of the things that matter to us, the interpretive lens through which we view the world is formed.

What matters on a person's agenda is finally a personal distillation from a mix of values, beliefs, relationships, goals, affective attachments, commitments, localities, and opportunities. One's interpretation of what's going on—for example, deciding that a particular set of facts comprises a problem that calls for attention and action—rests on these choices. However, new problems occur, new opportunities present themselves, new capabilities develop. Out of this reciprocal process emerges the list of things that need to be done and the interpretive framework within which we will make decisions about how to deal with that list.

Thus we come to the third function of the agenda: identifying the context in which we will respond to the expectations of the people who count about these things that matter. The basic premise of Niebuhr's model of human behavior is that all human behavior is a response to action upon us. At no time in our lives do we act first. We always make our choices in contexts that already exist, after choices have been made by others. We are never in a position to create the circumstances within which we act, or to act in isolation from the action of others. We respond to the expectations of others, albeit sometimes in creative and innovative ways.

So our decision making occurs in particular locations. Niebuhr's effort was to describe the "responsible self." We cannot simply be a responsible self, however, for the identity of each of us cannot be described adequately by the single concept "self." We are also parents, friends, citizens, Republicans, spouses, judges, students, Catholics, and many other things. Responsibility has a different content in each of these contexts. The meaning of "being responsible" can be articulated only as we understand that each of our responses takes place in the presence of various agendas. In the context of certain agendas we can define and prescribe the actions of, for example, a responsible parent or a responsible mayor. But that definition and prescription are dependent upon the expectations and structure provided by the specific context.

This description of human response seems to be applicable to all moral action. The word *moral* in this sense refers not to some acts as moral as opposed to immoral, but to acts that are moral as opposed to amoral—acts that are concerned with or have implications for matters of value. All moral acts contain the elements of response, interpretation, anticipation, and community.[7] These elements describe how individuals behave, how they live and choose, how they exist as humans.

What is missing is the ingredient that would enable us to move beyond this *description* of human action to a *prescription*—to a basis for giving answers to the question, "What ought I to do?" If every meaningful action is of this character, what is it that distinguishes one choice from another, an appropriate response from an inappropriate response? How do we determine what it means to be responsible in any given set of circumstances? While there is a certain intuitive appeal to this ethics of responsibility, its presentation by Niebuhr and others has lacked a concrete metaphor such as the images of pursuing goals or obeying rules that capture the alternative approaches to ethics. Responding to agendas can serve as a corresponding metaphor for a response ethic.

An individual enters each situation in which he or she acts, in which a response is elicited, with a personal history. From this history we bring with us a host of agendas, of things to be done. We all recognize the experience of feeling expectations about things we are to do: expectations of parents, teachers, friends, ministers, and such impersonalized societal forces as government and community. We may encounter a conflict between agendas, or even a conflict between items on the same agenda, and in that moment when the taken-for-granted action is no longer an automatic response, ethical reflection at some level is demanded.

Drawing upon this common experience, one way of viewing an ethics of responsibility is to see that acting responsibly is to follow an agenda. Our action is shaped by the agendas we have chosen and that have been chosen for us. Our response to others, our interpretation of particular actions upon us, our anticipation of future responses, and our choice of beings with whom to build community reflect the influence of the agendas that have a claim on us. It is as we accept a particular agenda, with its expectation of things to be done and the structure it brings to our lives, that we move toward filling in the missing ingredient that provides prescriptive substance for an ethics of responsibility.

There is no specific moral content to the notion of responsibility as such. We do, however, have a better sense of what it means to say that someone's actions should be appropriate to her role as a responsible accountant or that someone else's actions should be appropriate to his role as a responsible parent. Even this step, at first glance, seems to offer less guidance than a rule that dictates telling the truth or a goal of maximizing a child's welfare. Decisions about what is fitting in particular situations seem to rest on less solid ground, invoking some vague moral sense of judgment rather than clear statements of rules or goals. But this difference is illusory.

It is true that fashioning appropriate responses to the agendas we encounter entails a certain intuitive element. There is a moral judgment that is not reducible to applying a rule or calculating progress toward a goal. However, those who advocate views of the moral decision-making process that are seemingly more content-filled—who rely on specific rules or concrete goals—sooner or later employ the same, irreducibly moral, judgment. Consider, for example, a consequentialist who focuses on desired ends and believes that cost-benefit analysis provides an unerring moral compass. A host of questions arise that can only be answered, finally, by reference to some moral sense—whether it goes by the label of intuition or some other name. Which ends are good? How do you weigh the value of different goods? What counts as costs? How do you compare such incommensurable factors as the cost of increased death rates with the benefit of 10 percent cheaper electricity? How do you choose between contradictory cost-benefit calculations; which voices are to be heard? Indeed, why do you choose to value consequences over deontological considerations when many persons who have considered the options have chosen otherwise?

A similar list of questions exists, of course, for those who have chosen the person-as-citizen model over the person-as-maker model, beginning with: Why did you choose that approach? Which rules have you chosen to obey? Why are they authoritative? How do you reconcile conflicting interpretations of principles? How do you assign priorities among competing rules? In the same vein, if one chooses the kind of mixed approach described by Frankena, how do you decide when deontological principles override calculations of results?

At some point, the ethics of ends and the ethics of rules face the same deficiency as a response ethics. Moral decisions unavoidably are based on such fuzzy notions as discernment, intuition, personal judgment, moral sensitivity, discretion, conscience, or what Aristotle called "practical wisdom."[8] Albert Jonsen and Stephen Toulmin provide some insight into this reality as they relate the experience which led them to write *The Abuse of Casuistry.*[9]

Jonsen and Toulmin worked with the National Commission for the Protection of Human Subjects of Biomedical and Behavioral Research. The commission's charge was to review federal regulations with a concern to protect the "rights and welfare" of research subjects in biomedical or behavioral investigations. This task included developing general statements of ethical principles to serve as guides in the development of biomedical and behavioral research. The eleven commissioners came with widely varying backgrounds and interests. Given the diversity of the commission members—in terms of gender, race, religion, profession, political preferences, and philosophical commitments—little basis existed for expecting agreement on general moral principles or the application of them to particular problems. All the more striking, then, were Jonsen and Toulmin's observations that commission members generally agreed on specific practical recommendations. "Serious differences of opinion began to appear only when individual commissioners went beyond the stage of formulating practical propos-

als and explained their individual *reasons* for participating in the
collective recommendations."[10]

This story suggests that there may be something primary
about a practical understanding that recognizes the appropriate
course of action in a specific situation before general principles are
applied. As long as the commissioners focused on particular judgments, they saw things pretty much in the same way. What they
could not agree on was why they agreed. As soon as the conversation moved to the level of principles, they went their separate
ways. Their "locus of certitude" did not lie in a set of agreed-upon
principles but in a shared perception of what was at stake in particular human situations.

I am not suggesting an approach to ethics in which each
person simply looks at a situation, intuits the fitting responses, and
announces the conclusion without articulating supporting reasons.
Such a model would reduce ethical discourse to the level of the
childhood conversations that consist of two children merely yell-
ing back and forth, "Is too!" and "Is not!" Indeed, the discussion
above about the contribution of the metaphor of the agenda to a
response ethics indicates the kinds of reasons one would give—to
herself and to others—when ascertaining the appropriate response.
Conversations about who counts, what matters, and the context of
decision making would still take place. Principles would appear in
such discussions of reasons, but they would play a less tyrannical
role than when moral decisions are viewed as deductions from
established rules or outputs from cost-benefit calculations.

A distinctive ingredient in an ethics of responsibility and
in the model of responding to agendas is the communal nature of
the ethical decision-making process. Rather than mechanically applying formal rules or narrowly pursuing rigid goals, we respond to
myriad influences, values, and facts, as these are presented and
interpreted to us by other people. Carol Gilligan, in her book *In a
Different Voice,*[11] has given eloquent expression to this view of
moral choice. She writes that women have been socialized to attend to voices other than their own in making moral decisions.
Their moral strength, she argues, is found in an overriding concern
with relationships and responsibilities, growing out of an understanding of morality in which the moral problem is conflicting
responsibilities. The moral dilemma is how to lead a life that includes obligations to a host of different people and communities.

The road to resolution of this dilemma lies in a connection of the self to others, responding in recognition of the fact that others are counting on one who is in a position to help.

This listening to other voices, this acting on the basis of shared norms and values that sustain relationships in communities, is at the heart of an ethics of responsibility. The notion of the agenda is a particularly good way to understand this approach to moral choice. The act of putting an item on an agenda does not usually dictate certain action.[12] Rather it is an invitation to discussion, to raise your voice and hear other voices. Action on agenda items comes after more information has been gathered, after opinions have been shared and alternatives explored. An agenda item identifies a topic that must be addressed and acted upon. The specific action, however, flows from dealing with that topic with other people in a particular context.

Jonsen and Toulmin recover this notion from the tradition of casuistry. For the casuists, they write, the primary concern of informed conscience "was to place the individual agent's decision into its larger context at the level of actual choice: namely, the moral dialogue and debate of the community."[13] In this tradition, there was still a place for taking up personal moral positions in marginal or ambiguous cases, but only after a dialogue in which the meanings of the shared values of the group for a particular problem had been aired and duly considered.

For Alasdair MacIntyre, human transactions occur in conversations. Because conversation requires more than one person, and because each statement in a conversation is related to what has gone before and what will come after, this image helps us avoid the tendency to view life as a sequence of individual actions and episodes.[14] We create our own stories, but only as coauthors. We find our identity and create our personal agendas in and through the communities that surround us. This task is complicated in a culture in which, as MacIntyre describes it, the language of morality is in a state of grave disorder. But the remedy for such disorder is not to abandon conversation but to get better at it.

One potential problem with the use of the agenda metaphor for moral decision making is the apparent emphasis on what a self *does* at the expense of considering who the self *is*. Who I am and what I do are not, of course, unrelated. Our images of ourselves carry with them expectations of how we will act. To have a per-

sonal agenda is to have expectations of how we will typically respond to the'world. This notion is very much akin to one understanding of character: "[V]irtue and character refer to the typical
way we respond to problems, pursue purposes, and relate to other
people—not to Benjamin Franklin's checklist of individual moral
accomplishments."[15] The shaping of a personal agenda will be
formed by images of who I perceive myself to be—the good hus-
band, the bad boy, a free spirit, the victim, the faithful servant, and
so on.[16] Expectations that don't fit this self-image will be discarded
or create a crisis of identity.

The use of the notion of agendas to clarify an ethics of
response is one way to avoid the overly rigid styles that arise in
other approaches. The test in the rules approach is disobedience: a
person either follows the right rule or she doesn't. The test in the
goals approach is deviance: an individual either acts in pursuit of
the correct goals or he doesn't. A discussion of responses to agendas embodies nuances of difference that lead to a richer, more
textured understanding of moral action. When my response does
not fully match institutional expectations, that response might be
characterized in a variety of ways: as a total or partial withdrawal
from the institution; a limitation in the acknowledged scope of the
institutional agenda; an effort to reform the corporate agenda,
maybe even calling it to be truer to itself; a subversion of the group
in light of other claims; a reinterpretation of the institutional
agenda; an independent judgment about how specific, legitimate
expectations may be translated into action. As we look at types of
responses to agendas in part 2 we will explore these and other
possibilities, reminding ourselves that moral questions can rarely
be reduced to either/or options.

The Moral Force of Agendas

Agendas are comprised of things we are expected to do.
The previous section indicates how those expectations affect our
actions, how we take agendas into account when making our decisions. If agendas fit into our decision-making process in this way,
there still exists the additional issue of determining that the content of a particular agenda *should* be given weight as we form our
responses.

Without attempting to develop a comprehensive view of

the source of moral obligation, I can at least indicate the connection I see between agendas and moral choice. The general model of moral obligation I find persuasive is the membership model presented by Michael Walzer in *Obligations: Essays on Disobedience, War, and Citizenship*.[17] For Walzer, obligation has its source in membership, and "real obligation" arises when membership becomes willful in some sense of the term—even if it only means continued membership after a certain age. In his view, moral obligation is obligation to other people. Commitments to principles are usually commitments to other people—those from whom or with whom the principles have been learned, those who enforce the principles, those who benefit from the advancement of the principles. Obligation is thought of, then, not as pertaining to certain ideals, certain rules to be followed or goals to be pursued. It is rather a claim upon us by other people, and we must decide which of those persons is authoritative for us as we make our moral decisions.

Our membership, and especially our willing membership, in certain groups is the source of the expectations created by agendas. It is within particular groups or social institutions that we encounter agendas and their expectations about the issues and causes we should consider, the persons whose views we should take into account, and the context within which we should fashion a response. As I accept a position in an institution I am acknowledging that the expectations embedded within that institution's agenda make a legitimate claim on me. Such expectations exist in all social institutions.

Some examples provide clear illustrations. If I accept an office in which I promise to uphold and defend the Constitution of the United States, the citizens of that nation have a legitimate expectation that I will do so. If I participate in marriage and promise to honor and respect my wife, she has good reason to expect me to do so. These kinds of promises create new institutional settings or change the agendas of existing institutions. In so doing, they create new obligations.

Ethicists sometimes ponder the nature of our moral duty to tell the truth. Truth-telling expectations reflect a corporate context in which we all participate: the human race. The general expectation of truth-telling can be related to the maintenance of civilized society. This broad agenda gives way, however, to agendas that exist in smaller institutional settings, such as games, negotiations, national security discussions, international diplomacy. Sometimes the specialized agenda clearly overrides the more general set of expectations (e.g., a game in which deceit and discovery are the essence of the contest). In other cases, the clash between the divergent agendas yields conflicting judgments (e.g., whether a president should lie to the press to preserve the secrecy of a special mission to China). The point is that the actor's social location is always relevant in making judgments about moral obligations.

We live in the midst of myriad agendas. Our membership in groups and institutions, especially our willing membership, gives rise to expectations—expectations that we judge to be legitimate—that those corporate agendas will count as we decide what we ought to do. We cannot in every case follow those institutional agendas since we inevitably face legitimate expectations that conflict with one another. It does seem appropriate, however, to consider these legitimate expectations to be obligatory in a prima facie sense: that we should follow that agenda unless other moral considerations, legitimate contrary agendas, intervene.

In actual practice, more general expectations will usually present less intensely felt obligations than those based on more narrow, immediate relations. When agendas collide, it is understandable that the expectations developed in face-to-face encounters, those that arise from engagements intentionally forged, would elicit more commitment than those expectations arising from larger, more impersonal communities in which a more casual membership may have developed—perhaps more through default than explicit agreement. Good reasons can be given for drawing a correlation between the closeness of relationships and the strength of obligations in those relationships. The degree of closeness is influenced by such factors as benefit one has received, the prospects of helping another, mutual projects undertaken, and unilateral commitments that have been made.[18]

Moral obligation thus arises through our relationships with others. Responsible action is that which is appropriate in the context of those relationships, which fits with the legitimate expectations embodied in our life's agendas. Ethical reflection is prompted when conflicts arise among those expectations. Of special interest in this discussion is the conflict between personal agendas (those that we identify as ours, that we feel that we have chosen) and institutional agendas—which can be described for our purposes as those that are perceived as presenting expectations that we encounter as external demands. Such external demands are transmitted to us in a variety of ways. We may be faced with something as commanding as a draft notice from the Selective Service or as subtle as commonly practiced manners at a dinner table. These institutional agendas feel like they have been chosen for us by virtue of our membership in corporate bodies, and we must understand something of the nature of life within those corporate bodies to make informed judgments about our resolution of these conflicts. Thus we now turn to the culture of institutions and their agendas.

3

The Institutional Context

We live our lives as parts of social institutions. We are members of families, social clubs, civic organizations, and political groups. We work for companies, go to schools, and belong to churches and synagogues. We are citizens, responsible to city, county, state, and national governments. Every social institution of which we are a part holds out an agenda (often multiple agendas) for us. While we interpret what those corporate agendas mean in light of our own values and beliefs, they will never wholly match our personal agenda.[1] A problem arises not when the agendas are simply different—in which case they may be complementary or addressing different issues—but when they conflict, when adhering to one set of expectations would be detrimental to following another.

I want to emphasize a very important point, one that readers might tend to forget in the pages that lie ahead. This book may unduly put institutions in a bad light because it focuses on occasions of conflict. We should not forget that many times institutional and personal expectations are harmonious, and institutions can undergird, support, and enhance our personal agendas. In many instances, indeed if we have chosen wisely in the overwhelming majority of instances, the presentation of a corporate expectation will reinforce our personal values. Even in cases in which we think we have found a conflict, additional reflection can lead us to conclude there is no problem, and we move on, affirming both agendas. This congruity of individual and group norms is very important, but it is not the focus of this book.

Institutional Demands and Personal Choice

Since we frequently encounter this inevitable conflict between corporate and personal agendas, it is helpful to recall why we participate in social institutions. ("Corporate" as used here and elsewhere in this book refers not only to big business, but to any institution or associated group of persons.) We do not put ourselves into all institutions; often we are placed into them. We are born into a family and under the laws of existing governments. We live in neighborhoods, associate with peer groups, and take our assigned places in organizations. We join teams, clubs, and societies. Human beings are social creatures, through and through. As such, we make our way in this world only as parts of larger groups. Any thoughts of a world without institutions are illusory, for there can be no such place for humans.[2]

Life in the modern world in particular is marked by the abstract systems embedded in large institutions. Increasingly our lives are shaped by impersonal organizations rather than intimate associations. This feature of our existence has prompted Anthony Giddens to describe our lives as a ride on a juggernaut—a runaway engine of enormous power which we can drive to some extent, but which also threatens to rush out of our control:

> The juggernaut crushes those who resist it, and while it sometimes seems to have a steady path, there are times that it veers away erratically in directions we cannot foresee. The ride is by no means wholly unpleasant or unrewarding; it can often be exhilarating and charged with hopeful anticipation. But, so long as the institutions of modernity endure, we shall never be able to control completely either the path or the pace of the journey.[3]

Social institutions, however, are more than structures into which we are forced as a condition of survival. We enter many corporate settings voluntarily and remain in others after the compulsion of absolute necessity has passed. Sometimes this group membership is what Giddens calls a "bargain with modernity," less a conscious act of commitment than a tacit acceptance in which other possibilities are largely foreclosed.[4] On other occasions, however, we knowingly and willingly subject ourselves to institutional agendas that stray from and occasionally even attack our private notions of what is right and good. But why?

A social institution is more than the sum of the people who are affiliated with it. People come and go in an organization, but the organization remains. What remains in the midst of this coming and going is the institutional agenda. The specific content of such agendas changes, of course, but a recognizably continuing institutional agenda persists or the institution ceases to exist. Every institution has its list of things to be done and the procedures that have been developed to do those things. We recognize particular institutions because they have certain functions or purposes, certain agendas without which they can be considered no longer to exist. We know what schools are about. If we found that a school was using children on an assembly line to produce widgets rather than holding classes, we would conclude that a different institution had taken over the school's name, building, and personnel, replacing the no longer existing school. We know and recognize institutions by the group expectations they develop and follow.

To a large extent, we internalize the values and standards of the social institutions we inhabit. This is especially true of the more basic institutions in which we have participated throughout our lives. It is also the case that we have joined the institutions we have chosen later in life because of the appeal those agendas hold for us. Nevertheless, conflict between personal and corporate agendas is inevitable. One is rarely, if ever, completely socialized into a particular group's morality, and no single institutional arrangement will conform to all of the various components that make up an individual's agenda.

Our participation in any organization will limit our freedom to respond to the world in ways we think appropriate. Institutional structures and cultures shape our interpretation of situations and our definitions of problems. Institutional responsibilities and obligations will demand certain choices that we would otherwise not make. On the other hand, we find ourselves within these corporate settings because those institutions promote values and ends that we endorse. Our ability to advance particular items on our own agendas is enhanced by the use of institutional power.

This brings us to the basic dilemma that confronts each of us as we assess our involvement in social organizations. These institutions are valuable to us in different ways. Some institutions nurture us, educate us, offer us companionship. Others allow us to influence our political, economic, or social environment in ways that we never could as single individuals. We want to extend the reach of some institutions, to enhance their ability to serve their agendas, so that they will meet their charges effectively, competently, economically, efficiently. At the same time, we are safeguarding a value that sometimes is seen as contradictory to these effect-oriented considerations. We often want to restrain the reach of institutions as they infringe upon our freedom. In these cases, we want the effectiveness of institutions to be limited by our concerns for responsiveness, accountability, and personal choice.

To the extent that the maximization of an institution's agenda also promotes our personal agenda, we want the organization to be given the power and resources needed to pursue that agenda effectively and competently. When institutional activities begin to conflict with our own sense of what is appropriate, then we want to rein in the organization, limiting the extent to which it follows paths that we would not freely choose.

The tension between effectiveness and freedom is a commonly recognized theme in discussions of large-scale organizations. The most efficient organizations are often those that allow the least room for personal choice. Conformity to group norms reduces the time and energy drained away by debate, indecision, consultation, negotiation, and dissent. Less often recognized is the fact that institutional constraints are justified not only because they increase the effectiveness with which agendas can be addressed corporately, but also because they enhance the individual's ability to choose. Such structures often stand between freedom and chaos.

If each of us had to develop our personal agenda in a vacuum, the burden of choice would be so overwhelming that choice would be impossible. The manner in which institutional structures channel and direct our thoughts and activities is not always antithetical to free personal choice. At times, the restraints of a corporate setting are necessary to enable us to make real choices. We develop a personal agenda through a process of limiting available options, of reviewing alternative possibilities and discarding many while choosing a few. The guidance of institutional agendas, many of which are with us from birth, is what makes this task manageable.

The Rules of the Game

Some commentators analyze life in institutional settings by comparing that realm of human activity with the way we play games, in particular, with the rules that define the games and dictate how players are to behave. If the reality I have called an institutional agenda is recast as a set of institutional rules, and these rules are thought of in the same way that we think of the rules of chess or baseball, then we get a very different feel for the problem of conflicting moralities. Indeed, if this view of institutional rules were broadly accepted there would be little place for a book such as this one.

Albert Carr has written one of the classic essays advocating this rules-of-the-game approach to business ethics.[5] Carr recognizes that the conflicting pulls of personal morality and institutional expectations can inflict grave psychological strain and dislocation in family life for the person caught in the middle. He sees the source of the problem, however, in the individual's failure to understand that there should *not* be any such conflict. What appear to be unethical institutional demands are actually justified by the fact that life in such institutions has the impersonal character of a game, a game with a special ethical code.

An illustration Carr uses is of a fifty-eight-year-old man who sold advertising space in a magazine and found himself out of a job. His chances of getting a new job were diminished by his age. He and his wife decided he could pass for forty-five, and he put that age on his résumé. Knowing that the truth about his age might eventually come out, he concluded that he could handle that development when the time came. Carr's conclusion: "This was a lie; yet within the accepted rules of the business game, no moral culpability attaches to it."[6]

Carr found no moral culpability because he views the ethics of business as game ethics. The business game has its own standards of right and wrong, standards that are different from the prevailing traditions of morality in our society. According to this view, no one should think any worse of the game of business because its standards are different. Once people become game players, they must be guided by this different set of ethical expectations.

Carr draws an analogy to the game of poker. Poker has its own brand of ethics. It calls for distrust of others. It ignores claims of friendship; cunning deception and concealment are vital in the game, not kindness and open-heartedness. No one expects poker to be played according to the moral principles preached in the churches, and no one thinks any the worse of poker on that account. And just as there exist rules of the game that govern how poker players behave, so there are rules to business and other institutional enterprises that are to be followed without concern for external ethical standards that simply do not apply.

Seen in this light, one could say that persons who are troubled about disparities between personal and institutional agendas don't understand the character of institutional life. The institutions have their own ethics, their own sets of rules just as games have their own rules. Game players, members of institutions, need only master the rules of the game and ignore their private ethical standards and personal feelings. Thus, there would be no conflicts between personal and institutional agendas.

There are three difficulties with this rules-of-the-game escape from the problem of conflicting agendas. First, the institutional standards that Carr describes are not analogous to what we mean by rules of a game, but rather to what we think of as winning strategies. Second, the analogy between institutional expectations and game-winning strategies is tenuous because of the vast difference in the character of games and social life. Third, the similarities that do exist between game playing and institutional life actually serve to reinforce the view that the conflict between personal and corporate agendas is a serious problem we must address.

First, what is the purpose of game rules? The rules indicate the boundaries that separate the game from a wider context, defining which actions are and which are not part of the game.[7] Rules do not tell us what actions we *ought* to perform to play a game; they tell us what actions *must* be performed to play a game. A disregard for the rules means that I am not playing the game.

Suppose a friend challenged me to a softball game, inviting me to round up a group of players and meet at a designated time and place. If I show up with eleven players and we proceed to line up along the left field foul line, kick a football into the outfield and then tackle the center fielder who picks it up, my friend could rightly argue that I was not playing softball. The rules of the game are binding on softball players and other game players in a tautological sense. If I don't abide by softball rules, I am not a softball player. The rules of softball do change, and the softball rules in one locality or level of play may differ from those in another. But each time a softball game is played there is a mutually agreed upon set of rules that are followed, or there is no softball game.

Those who attempt to apply the game-rules approach to business and other corporate endeavors mean something very different. The rules they discuss are not those that define who, for example, is doing business or conducting diplomacy, but rather the rules they think *should* guide those who want to do well in business or to conduct diplomacy successfully. For Carr, the consequence of not following the rules of the game is not that one will cease to be a business executive, but that one will not accumulate much money or power.[8] The institutional rules of the game are really not such rules at all but rather guides to a winning strategy. I can choose not to follow such suggestions and still continue to be a business executive. The important phrase in the preceding sentence is, "I can choose." With this realization, the ploy of the business-as-a-game approach fails. Despite efforts to characterize business strategies as reality-defining rules which of necessity must be followed by those in the business, it is clear that this automatic abdication of the participants' moral sensibilities cannot be so easily presumed.

As we have discussed, corporations and other institutions do have specialized codes of conduct, which I have characterized as institutional agendas. These group expectations are often distinct from personal moral standards. But if an analogy between institutional life and games is to be of any use in understanding the former, the analogy must be drawn between the ethics of business (or politics or family relations) and gamesmanship—not the rules of the game itself.

Second, even the analogy between these institutional rules and winning strategies or gamesmanship is tenuous because of the dissimilarities between game playing and social life. A game is an artificially limited situation. The rules allow players to calculate with certainty the consequences that will flow from particular happenings. People choose whether or not they want to play. The rules are clearly defined and known to all before the game begins, and they don't change in the middle of the game, except by mutual consent. The risks are limited; players can quit without far-reaching consequences for the rest of their lives. In a game, there is a single goal to be achieved: to win.

Real life is not game playing. Dorothy Emmett has pointed to the complexity of real life as a basic source for understanding the difference between moral principles and the rules of games. Games are purposefully set up, she argues, so that there are not rules that require that moves be made in conflicting ways at the same time. One may be in doubt about the best move to make among those that are permitted, but no rule is broken in choosing one or the other. She views moral directives in a different light: "[I]n real-life situations it is perfectly possible for there to be situations to which several principles are applicable, and it is only possible to keep one at the cost of breaking another. This is because principles do not form a single pattern in the way in which rules of a game do, and because, in real life, situations are not artificially limited so that these conflicts do not arise."[9]

Life in a corporation, political party, religious denomination, or family is simply not like playing a game. While games engage us (at our option) in very limited, focused ways, we are forced to interact constantly in institutional settings in ways that profoundly affect our well-being and the health and happiness of our loved ones. The stakes are raised and the controls released as we move from the game situation to the real world and, as a result, the pertinence of gamesmanship fades.

Gamesmanship involves the use of methods that seem improper but that are not strictly illegal. Such a definition fits quite well with the strategies Carr uses as illustrations of playing by business rules in his article: using deceptive packaging, outdated actuarial tables (to gain higher premium payments), or misleading advertising; or manufacturing products deleterious to health. Carr judges such examples of entrepreneurial gamesmanship in this way: "As long as they comply with the letter of the law, they are within their rights to operate their businesses as they see fit."[10]

How well does this gamesmanship analogy fit into institutional life? The parallel with business may seem appropriate to some observers. In a game, the players have the single goal: to win. In business, according to some analysts, the players also have a single goal: to make money. In each case, the players would be justified in pursuing any winning strategy that is legal. Some views of a corporate agenda, however, reject this argument. Consider, for example, the following statements which are among the stated objectives of the Dow Chemical Company:

> To seek maximum long-term profit growth as the primary means to insure the prosperity of our employees and stockholders, the well-being of our customers, and the improvement of people's lives everywhere. . . . To practice stewardship in the manufacture, marketing, use and disposal of our products. To share in the responsibility of all peoples for protection of the environment. To make wise and efficient use of the earth's energy and natural resources. To make this world a better place for our having been in business.[11]

The cynic will look at such corporate statements and label them rhetorical window dressing, seeing their purpose to be only enhancing the company's public image in order to increase profits. The hard question is whether a business ever makes decisions for the sake of the environment or social justice rather than considering only the financial cost or benefit to the institution. Other institutions clearly engage in such reasoning (for example, universities divesting their South African holdings) and anecdotal evidence suggests that businesses may occasionally do the same.

Putting aside for a moment the appropriateness of the rules-of-the-game analogy for business, how would this single-minded approach work in other areas? In some segments of society, it is impossible to develop a single criterion by which to measure institutional success. What is the single goal governing the choosing of strategies by parents or rabbis or neighbors or leaders of professional societies? In other areas, we do have cases that more closely resemble the business world—at least insofar as a sole indicator of success can be paramount. But I find myself very uncomfortable with justifying strategies in those areas that lead to success, without regard for other costs. Is it acceptable that, within the bounds of legality, students are urged to do anything they can to earn the highest grades? Do we want the only consideration of our political leaders to be winning the next election? Do we want research scientists to think about anything other than the size of the next research grant they can win? In short, do we care about societal and human costs, as long as the trains run on time?

One answer is that we should enact into law any of the

basic societal rules that currently exist in ethical custom if we want those rules to be followed—an option I find unfeasible and undesirable. Another answer is that the gamesmanship analogy is appropriate only for some institutional settings, maybe only for the business world. By revisiting Carr's essay one more time, however, we can see that the similarities that do exist between games and business reinforce the notion that personal morality continues to play a prominent role, even in games and analogous situations.

The *unethical* poker player, Carr tells us, "finds a way to put the other player at an unfair disadvantage. Perhaps he unnerves them with loud talk. Or he tries to get them drunk. Or he plays in cahoots with someone else at the table. Ethical poker players frown on such tactics."[12] There is nothing, of course, in the rules of the game of poker that proscribe these kinds of strategies. The game has no rules to tell us which disadvantages are "unfair." What, then, is the source of Carr's judgment that bluffing is ethical but unnerving an opponent with loud talk is not? Why is it not ethical for a poker player to do everything possible, within the rules, to win— just as Carr tells us it is ethical for business executives to do everything possible within the law to make a larger profit?

It is at this point that Carr's analogy breaks down completely. Although poker is played by a set of rules, Carr obviously thinks that moral judgments should be made about ethical and unethical playing, judgments that are not based on the rules of the game. He makes distinctions between ethical and unethical poker players without acknowledging that he has brought his own personal moral standards into the analysis. In the end, he is not willing to approve any tactics that are within the rules of the game. If he is not willing to take such an approach to a poker game, how can he possibly expect us to take such an approach to the world of business?

Personal morality enters into even as carefully limited a world as a poker game. And if the players in a poker game invariably call upon their personal agendas, so much more so will players in schools, families, churches, civic organizations, professional associations, and corporations. Personal agendas play a role in institutional settings in at least the following ways: (1) institutional agendas have their source, in part, from the personal agendas of those who have been and are members of the institutions; (2) the interpretation and understanding of the meaning of institutional agendas are shaped by the personal agendas of the individuals involved; (3) decisions about changing or disregarding institutional agendas, or about leaving institutions entirely, are informed by personal agendas.

The point in dispute is not whether the moral choices of individuals are influenced or formed by the institutional settings within which they act. Indeed, the observation that such an influence exists is the point of departure for this entire enterprise. The question raised by the rules-of-the-game approach is whether some institutional settings are immune to the considerations of ordinary morality that receives its expression in our personal agendas. If this were to be the case, then the problem of conflicting agendas would cease to be a problem in those institutions. The affirmation here, however, has been the contrary: the character of institutional life is such that the conflict cannot be defined out of existence. We must continue to grapple with the problem, each of us taking responsibility for finding our own resolution.

Living in Groups

We encounter as many corporate agendas as there are social institutions. Sometimes an institution's list of things for us to do can helpfully deflect certain demands upon us (for example, "I don't do windows"). Other times, such an agenda prohibits us from pursuing a desirable course of action (for example, "I am truly sorry, but that's out of my hands"). One common feature of corporate agendas is that they contain institutional expectations that define a community of personal interaction and a set of norms and values to which our behavior is to conform.

Within the corporate setting, an institution's agenda—or agendas—comes to us as in many different ways: as direct orders by those in authority; by our new discovery of what must be done to carry out an order, even though that action was not a part of the formal command; in official or unofficial job descriptions; through an understanding that all members or participants are to act in ways that serve the institution's goals—stated and unstated; in an informal network of individuals who interact with one another and evolve a shared set of expectations; through institutional traditions and customs that pass down the lore as it has developed over time. This list could be lengthened and each item on it subdivided.

Whether we are an employee, a student, a stockholder, a member of a political party, church, or club, we receive these messages describing things to be done.

Life in a corporate setting is rarely so simple that we are presented with a single organizational agenda. For example, the institution's mission might convey one set of expectations to you, while stated goals and objectives might convey a second set, and actual policies and procedures a third. The corporate situation is complicated by the possibility of differences between official institutional missions and the needs or desires of institutional elites to perpetuate or reproduce their hierarchical dominance and command of resources. Even the concept of an institutional agenda that is not mediated by interested and biased parties seems to be a fiction. Thus, the ideal of an institution marked by rationality, intentional action, and a reasonable organization of means and ends has given way to a view of institutions as being marked by competition, coercion, conflict, power, and bargaining.[13] We never respond to one institutional agenda, but to various, at times competing, representations of the corporate agenda.

While our experience with corporate agendas is complex and diverse, the ways that corporate agendas come to us can be summarized as through: (1) formal systems; (2) informal interaction; and (3) external requirements. In a *formal* system, our response is to an institutional agenda that is primarily communicated to us in commands that come through a bureaucratic hierarchy. This kind of system is characterized by rigid kinds of authority with specified channels of communication. We interpret the commands we receive in light of the formal rules and practices that exist in the administrative arena. Our accountability is to identifiable superiors and can be traced along the lines of an organizational chart. In such a system, authority is based on some formal document, such as bylaws, and is enforced by a set of rules that are legitimated by their adherence to those bylaws. The military, certain large corporations, and the more hierarchical ecclesiastical bodies contain elements of the formal communication of expectations. In such a system, power and authority are closely linked.[14]

In this type of system, the institutional agenda is usually clear, or more precisely, the mediator of the agenda is usually clear. When one is considering affiliation with such an institution, it is usually easy at the outset and in each step along the way to weigh the corporate agenda against one's personal agenda. Despite some lack of consistency between the agenda implicit in the official institutional norms and the behavior actually sanctioned and expected in practice, the authority responsible for articulating the agenda that is in effect in a particular set of circumstances can generally be identified.

For a person who discovers a conflict between a corporate agenda and a personal agenda this type of system may seem inflexible. The flow of information is more likely to be one way—from the top down—producing a sense of impotence in the face of the institutional imperatives. This type of situation presents one with the feeling of being a cog in a machine.

Life in an *informal* system is different. Despite the orders and commands that exist within an administrative system, communication also will come informally, bypassing formal channels. Interpreting the corporate agenda may take place in the terms of informal expectations and arrangements that have developed in addition to written policies. Accountability often bypasses the hierarchy or can run off the organizational chart—or there may not even be a hierarchy or organizational chart. Loyalties within the institution may be more determined by friendships and personal styles and interests than by official status.

In such a setting, communication of the institutional agenda will likely take place on a more ad hoc basis. A presentation of the institution's agenda more often will be tailored to particular issues at hand than to formal charter-type documents. Our sense of expectations is shaped by the images and stories and myths that communicate institutional values. Authority may be based more on tradition than on legal documents, and power may be a function of charisma. Families and neighborhood groups are dominated by the informal process, and pockets of this type of interaction can be found in even the most formal, hierarchical organizations.

In this kind of informal setting, there is less certainty about what one will be asked to do. The agenda often will be set by an individual within the system rather than by some formal organizational mechanism. In smaller organizations, which are almost inevitably less formal, loyalty seems to be directed more toward individuals than toward the institution. As compared to a formal system, this kind of arrangement seems to offer more opportunities to incorporate personal agendas into organizational activities. In fact, however, the lack of clarity about the institutional agenda can create an unstable situation in which limits to increasing institutional demands are not clear.

Third, an institution's agenda can derive from *external* sources. If one assumes that an institution is subject to the law, professional or technical standards, or some other external criteria, then certain items on a corporate agenda are communicated to its members from these sources outside the institution. In this way, for example, an employee responds to the corporate agenda as she acts in accord with the specialized framework in which she has been trained. This person sees herself as accountable to her vocational ideals and professional canons and grants a certain authority to her fellow professionals. University professors and physicians are two examples of professionals who interpret their institutional obligations within the broader context of professional obligations. Similarly, persons can appropriately see themselves as responding to institutional expectations as they act in ways that conform to governmental executive orders or legislative decrees. Indeed, a nation of laws will continue to be a nation of laws only as group members make some assumption that group expectations typically stay within legal boundaries.

Institutional agendas shaped by external forces may be the most difficult to read. There are many sources and many interpreters of outside influences on groups. The legitimacy of an external expectation can always be questioned in light of internal expectations or competing external norms. Many private clubs and organizations, for example, continue to struggle with the degree to which societal concerns with racism, sexism, and heterosexism should alter their institutional agendas.

No corporate setting matches any one of these types, nor does this brief typology embrace all of the ways in which one can discover the content of an institutional agenda. Institutions vary greatly in their dispersal of authority, distribution of rights, degree and rigidity of hierarchical structure, claims made on members, and internal traditions and norms. We should not underestimate the pressure individuals face to be loyal to institutions and adhere to the corporate agenda. We confront a "stacked deck"[15] in which relationships have been structured in a way that group members will typically choose the institution's preferred way of doing things. People are taught that there is no salvation outside a particular church. Employees get "bought," finding it too expensive to leave the business. Strong social disapproval of divorce has created incentives to stay in marriages, no matter how miserable the relationships become. The state's police power is used to keep people in line.

Institutions exert such a strong influence in shaping our behavior that we often find ways of blurring the tension between personal and institutional agendas by blurring any sense of personal responsibility within institutions. Two such devices for evading personal responsibility are the concepts of hierarchical responsibility and collective responsibility.[16] The first concept provides us with a model in which responsibility falls on the person who stands highest in the chain of authority. The second is built on a view that each person's contribution is so small and so indistinguishable from the contributions of others, that either everyone is responsible or only the collective body is responsible.

The outcome for these two models is the same: no one is personally responsible. The hierarchical model yields a person at the top who steps forward and says, "The buck stops here." In many cases, however, everyone knows that the person at the top was so distanced from the actual decisions and behavior that the acceptance of responsibility is little more than a meaningless ritual relieving those down the ladder of responsibility. The result for the collective model is the same. If everyone is responsible, then no one is. A theory of responsibility that ignores such basic questions as who acted or failed to act, who had pertinent knowledge, or who was in a position to affect an outcome is meaningless.

Only when individuals are held accountable for the personal choices they make will the concept of responsibility have any force in an institutional context. The notion of personal accountability means that when confronted with institutional expectations individuals must reflect on their choices, weigh their alternatives, and make their decisions. This process of reflection and action will be informed and shaped by their personal agendas. The focus of this book is on personal responses when those institutional expectations conflict with those personal agendas. We now turn to the discussion in part 2 of the strategies that are available as we face that inevitable conflict between institutional expectations and personal agendas.

Part II

Personal Responses to Institutional Agendas

4

The Hermit

As explained in the Introduction, the chapters in part 2 will present a typology of personal responses to institutional agendas. This examination will clarify or describe the range of options available to a person faced with conflicting personal and institutional standards.

The Roman procurator Pontius Pilate chose to wash his hands of the decision regarding the fate of Jesus of Nazareth. Eduard Shevardnadze resigned as foreign minister when he believed that he could not support the domestic policies being pursued by Mikhail Gorbachev. Offended by the political and economic realities of American society, Henry David Thoreau took a two-year leave of absence on the shore of Walden Pond in Concord, Massachusetts. One personal response to institutional agendas has been to withdraw—from a particular decision, an institution or a community.

The "hermit" exemplifies the extreme forms of withdrawal by choosing to live in seclusion, removed from social contact and activity. Disengagement can occur on three different levels. First, when the gap between personal and societal agendas becomes too wide and the weight of social expectations too great, a person may choose to drop out, to prefer seclusion over membership in a community. Second, we may also separate or detach ourselves from institutional expectations in less sweeping ways. We resign offices, divorce spouses, change churches, quit jobs, and move to other communities. We can choose to exit particular institutions without taking the more extreme step of disaffiliating with society at large. Third, more partial responses to the separation impulse allow us to stay within an institution but to distance ourselves from particular activities or aspects of life within that institution—to qualify our membership in the group. People choose this tactic as a way of relieving themselves of responsibility for a specific item on an institutional agenda, thereby making more tolerable and acceptable the acknowledged divergence between institutional and personal norms.

This most limited form of disengagement typically is chosen when an individual is unalterably opposed to a specific policy or practice that is a significant item among the set of expectations mediated by that institution, but when continued membership in that corporate enterprise is, on the whole, still desirable. In such circumstances, she can make efforts to remove herself from participation in the particular matter in dispute but not from the whole institution. An illustration of such a choice at the national level comes from the Lyndon Johnson administration during the Vietnam War. Bill Moyers had so clearly distanced himself from the administration's Vietnam policy that the president is reported to have greeted his arrival at meetings with, "Well, here comes Mr. Stop-the-Bombing."[1] Moyers made it plain to all that in this instance he was not going to respond positively to expectations that policy-level officials support government policy. Yet his disaffection was not so broad as to lead him to resign.

In those war years it was not uncommon to see citizens refusing to say the pledge of allegiance to the American flag or to stand when the national anthem was played. These were statements of symbolic refusal to participate in the societal project although disaffection for such individuals was not great enough for them to choose to leave the country. When such activities are protest statements with some hope of bringing about change, these responses more properly fit the "reformer" type that is discussed in chapter 7. But as efforts to remove oneself from an aspect of an institutional agenda, these actions share the hermit's impulse to separate and distance oneself from the group expectations.

Many feminists, for example, have faced the tension of dealing with offensive expectations within religious institutions as they have advocated the ordination of women. Some have responded to patriarchal traditions by simply leaving the organized church. Others, however, have chosen a more partial withdrawal, taking steps to remove themselves from an association with that particular aspect of the institution. Thus, for example, women were "irregularly" ordained as Episcopal priests in the 1970s. Apart from whatever hope may have existed that the church would be reformed, the participants in this ceremony were making a statement: we love the church, we're staying in the church, but we are disassociating ourselves from the restrictions that have traditionally been imposed in this aspect of its institutional life.

Institutions sometimes develop structured ways of allowing for this partial withdrawal without a full departure from the corporate body. Members of organizations can ask that they be recorded as present but not voting when they wish to withhold even the assent that voting no implies for a particular proceeding. The United Way allows contributors to designate their gifts so that a pro-life donor can participate in the fund drive without directly supporting Planned Parenthood—even though Planned Parenthood has made clear that United Way funds are used for educational purposes, not the performing of abortions.

Judges recuse themselves from participating in cases when they cannot fulfill the institutional expectations that an impartial judgment be rendered. Supreme Court Justice Felix Frankfurter presented an interesting example of this practice when he removed himself from *Public Utilities Commission v. Pollak*. Noting that judges should think dispassionately, submerging private feelings, Justice Frankfurter concluded, "My feelings are so strongly engaged as a victim of the practice in controversy that I had better not participate in judicial judgment upon it."[2] The practice in question, of such national importance as to fill a slot on the Supreme Court's docket, was the playing of radio programs over speakers in public streetcars and buses in Washington, D.C.

At times it is possible to create "social enclaves" within institutions, relatively independent units within larger units that make individual choice more possible.[3] Such enclaves provide a buffer from the overwhelming power of large institutions for persons who want to retreat from the mainstream. Individuals who choose this limited form of disengagement are not, of course, literally doing what hermits do. They remain within the institution, active in much of its life. What they do share with the hermit is a nonnegotiable rejection of an institutional expectation. For this purpose, in light of this particular agenda item, they are going to the wilderness.

The next level of response, as we move up the scale of

disaffection, is to withdraw from an institution. At times the conflict between personal and corporate agendas is so great that continued membership becomes too problematic. It is interesting to note in this context that "resignation" has two meanings: (1) a submissive attitude, an unresisting acquiescence; and (2) the act of withdrawing, of giving up an office or position. The first definition could be thought of as withdrawing in spirit, as withholding one's investment in an active commitment to an institutional agenda. This type of response, however, is more suitably addressed under the types of the "institutionalized person" or the "split personality" in later chapters. The response that is true to the spirit of the hermit is one that in fact separates one from the organization in question.

Examples of leaving institutions are readily available in all areas of life. Teenagers run away from home. Soldiers desert. Officials and laborers quit their jobs. Customers take their business elsewhere. Priests turn in their orders. Democrats become Independents. In each instance one's sense of what it means to be faithful to her agenda requires that she break her ties with a particular group. Some forms of exiting are aggressive market choices (such as taking a higher-paying job) that do not fit the connotation of the hermit. The focus here is on those exits that do result from a hermitlike conclusion that one's values cannot be served in a particular setting.

We should recognize that withdrawing from an institution or a community is often a matter of transferring to a smaller, more homogenous group. While hermits can be isolated individuals, the route of withdrawal can also lead into cloistered communities or other smaller groups with agendas more akin to our own. This kind of movement entails not simply a decision to withdraw or not, but a weighing of the relative attractiveness of two different institutions.

The most complete form of the separation response occurs when one does what hermits do—withdraws from society to live in seclusion. In such cases, the need is not to escape a specific organization but to free oneself from societal expectations. Decisions to leave behind the conventional structure of society take place along a continuum of possibilities. At the extreme are those individuals who pack up and go into the wilderness, cutting off all contact with other human beings. An example would be our romanticized notion of the frontier mountain men, although many of them avoided pure solitude as they negotiated coexistence with Native Americans or made annual treks to civilization to sell furs. Located at different places along the spectrum between pure isolationists and fully participating societal members are a variety of recluses, solitaires, drop-outs, and other persons living, by choice or by chance, on the fringes of society. Another variation on this theme includes those who isolate themselves from society at large with a few chosen companions, such as those who choose to live in a monastery or an insular commune.

The hermit's response fits within the mode of individual adaptation that Robert Merton calls "retreatism": "People who adapt (or maladapt) in this fashion are, strictly speaking, *in* the society but not *of* it. Sociologically, these constitute the true aliens. Not sharing the common frame of values, they can be included as members of the *society* (in distinction from the *population*) only in a fictional sense."[4] The common thread running through these various possibilities is the escape from institutional expectations. The hermit's response to a clash of personal and institutional agendas is to resolve the conflict by negating the institutional claim on that person. The hermit's primary concern is not to change the institutional agenda but to separate from it, leaving those expectations intact but only for the others who are still associated with the group.

Helen Rose Fuchs Ebaugh's study of "exes," individuals who have chosen the hermit's option, focuses on voluntary withdrawal from particular social roles—ex-doctor, ex-convict, ex-cult member, retiree, divorcé, etc.[5] Her description of the process of role exit[6] includes both a disengagement from an institutional role (separation from an institutional agenda) and a reestablishment of one's identity (reshaping the personal agenda). The disengagement is a withdrawal from certain normative expectations that are no longer accepted as personally relevant. As one ceases to think of oneself in light of a particular institutional affiliation it is necessary to identify and embrace a new set of norms and expectations.

Two different impulses lead one to seek this kind of withdrawal. The motivation may come principally either from a judgment that the institutional agenda is bad or from a judgment that the personal agenda is good. While each choice is informed to some degree by both judgments, there does seem to be a difference in tone depending on whether one is acting primarily to escape from one reality or to move toward another. The rhetoric that accompanies one's choice often reflects whether one factor or the other is dominant.

Henry David Thoreau's words in "Civil Disobedience" convey the thoughts of one driven away from the state. Believing governments generally to be perverted, abused, and as likely to serve the devil as God, he wrote, "That government is best which governs not at all." One could not be associated with the American government in that day without disgrace, he believed, concluding, "I simply wish to refuse allegiance to the State, to withdraw and stand aloof from it effectually."[7] His disaffection extended beyond government to the economic realm ("trade curses everything it handles") and society in general, as he wrote of "the fancied advantages of human neighborhood" and his belief that "savage races" had been "degraded by contact with civilized man."[8]

Even in Thoreau's writing we find evidence of the lack of purity in human responses that prevents us from neatly categorizing them into one type or another. Thoreau qualified his statement about withdrawing from the state by adding that he intended still to "make use and get what advantage of her I can."[9] His statement in favor of separation, not to mention his actual implementation of that intention, reveals the compromising or ambivalent spirit that often leads us to "muddling through" rather than making clean, definitive judgments in response to conflicting agendas.

Thoreau saw the antithesis of the values he embraced in society and its institutions. This repulsion, this sense of being driven away from the existing social order, gave rise to one of the most famous anti-institutional statements in the English language: "If a man does not keep pace with his companions, perhaps it is because he hears a different drummer. Let him step to the music which he hears, however measured or far away."[10]

A more positive picture of the impulse to separation is painted by Maggie Ross, a contemporary religious solitary. Her language about the reason for withdrawal from mainstream social life is full of the good inherent in the hermit's choice rather than the perversion of the "normal" choice. She writes of being called into truth and confrontation with mercy, into a solitude that is "the meeting place with God." The attraction is to an opening of the heart to be aware of God at every moment in our deepest being[11] and an integrity that yields a morality that is not confused with popular opinion or the pressure of peer approval.[12] The emphasis is on what is being sought, not what is escaped.

For Ross, solitude is a matter of the heart and not limited to wilderness hermits: "You can have exterior solitude and not be in solitude at all because you have a cocktail party or a disco going on in your head. On the other hand, I've had some very solitary moments on the West Side IRT in Manhattan at rush hour."[13]

The important factor is not one's physical location but a state of mind, or of heart, which is attuned to the uniqueness that constitutes each person. Unique persons have unique agendas, not simply ones borrowed from groups and organizations. The hermit's response focuses on the unique personal agenda in a way that denies membership in—or fidelity to the expectations of—social institutions. Sometimes we actually separate ourselves from a group. Sometimes, dissatisfaction with an institutional agenda can lead to spiritual or mental withdrawal from a corporate body. We don't vote at election time. We quit going to meetings or stop talking to family members. We maintain formal membership, but just don't participate. We may be there in body, but that's all.

Let's recall the example described in the Introduction that will serve as a model throughout these chapters to illustrate the practical significance of each type. The case involves a young man, John, who, as part of his personal agenda, has developed an expectation that he will not discriminate against other persons because of their race or gender. However, John belongs to a private country club whose practices in accepting new members appear to discriminate against nonwhites, representing a conflict between personal and institutional agendas for John.

What would the hermit's response mean for John? The most obvious answer is that he would quit the club. If he found the conflict between his personal values and the club's agenda intolerable, and if he perceived little probability that the latter would change, he might simply leave. He would resolve the conflict between the agendas by withdrawing from the institution, thus freeing himself from any association with its agenda and negating any expectations it might place on him.

The more partial withdrawal might also be an option to consider, although exercising such a choice in this type of case might call into question John's commitment to his personal agenda.

He could withdraw from the membership selection process. If he saw the conflict between agendas to be restricted to how the club admitted new members, John could refrain from any participation in that process. In so doing, he might convince himself that he was not supporting, indeed was not even associated with, the aspect of the club that he found offensive. The question is whether this limited separation satisfactorily resolves the conflict, since John is still receiving benefits from and contributing to the support of a racially exclusive organization.

John's reflection on this conflict could push him toward the other end of the hermit's spectrum. Becoming fully aware of the prejudicial nature of the private country club, he could turn an investigatory eye toward other social institutions to which he belongs. He could discover a pattern of unfair treatment that offends him in the workplace, the political process, the educational system, religious institutions. In short, he may find the same conflict between his personal agenda and social expectations existing in a variety of institutions. If the offending agendas are pervasive and the prospect of reform slight, John could seek to remove himself from major sectors of society, seeking to reduce his personal benefit from unequal treatment of others and distancing himself from that society in an effort to diminish his contribution to those enterprises, as well as reduce his guilt by association.

The hermit's conviction is certainly attractive. Each of us wants to be our own person. There is little appeal in being a lackey in the service of others. We know the sorrow of seeing our vision of "the good life" being contaminated or shattered through our entanglements with institutions. But this response also presents problems for us. We are all products of social institutions and, with very rare exceptions, we all continue to depend on them for the support and even the definition of our unique selves. Those who too easily choose the hermit option may underestimate the extent to which we are entangled with our institutions. The result could be the desire acknowledged by Thoreau to "have it both ways," to disassociate ourselves from any institutional obligations while reaping institutional benefits. Groups can handle this benefits-but-no-burdens attitude among a limited number of their members; indeed, there are often institutional mechanisms which take this into account. For example, churches and other institutions which rely on voluntary contributions plan on a certain "shrinkage" when anticipating the conversion of pledges to actual cash received. The widespread adoption of this option, however, leads to the dissolution of those institutions. If too many pledges of financial support go unfilled, the institution dies. The obvious fact is that any institution ceases to exist when too many of its members choose to respond to group expectations by separating and withdrawing.

There are potential drawbacks to separation apart from losing the benefits of institutions or society. Those who do choose an isolation more like that associated with the hermit become somewhat immune to the moderating element inherent in recognizing the validity of social and public ideals. The reliance on one's personal agenda may produce admirable people of great integrity, but it may also produce people who are self-indulgent or socially irresponsible.[14] Included among our individual potentialities are weaknesses and destructive life-diminishing dispositions. The richness of our institutional traditions expands our moral horizons in ways that, we hope, will check the worst expressions of these vices. A departure from these traditions may increase the possibility of inappropriate choices that are self-absorbed or self-deluded.

As Carol Gilligan has observed, one problem with using "exit" as a paradigm for resolving conflicts is that it "obscures the reality of interdependence and masks the possibilities for cooperation."[15] Choosing separation can deny too quickly the possibilities of reform and improvement in institutions. These possibilities and the interplay between speaking out for change and leaving an institution will be discussed more fully under the type of the reformer (chapter 7). At this point our consideration of the hermit's option can benefit from Gilligan's observations about adolescents and their choices in a family.

The transformations of adolescence increase the potential for both exit and for speaking out in protest. The growth to puberty releases the child from dependence on parents and makes separation a more viable option as a solution to conflicts in the family. At the same time, the increasing availability of this option may make the adolescent more free in speaking out, in voicing views that diverge from accepted family truths. This coming to "voice" may affect the assessment of the alternative of separation: "In sum, adolescent girls who resist exit may be holding on to the position that solutions to dilemmas of attachment in adolescence must be forged by voice and that exit alone is no solution but an admission of defeat. Thus, their resistance may signify a refusal to leave before they can speak."[16]

Many observers of the modern scene think the temptation today is not that too many people will follow their personal agendas out of institutions, but rather that the pressures to conform are so great that people won't leave when they should. Alan Goldman identifies the central problem in professional ethics, as actually practiced, as the professionals' assumption that they should live up to such institutional expectations as official codes and professional principles, without question.[17] The path of least resistance is to maintain group memberships and match the institutional expectations of loyalty. Often our tendency is not to abandon a group too quickly, but to run with the crowd too long.

If we are aware of these tendencies in ourselves, then we should be especially vigilant about unintentionally straying from our personal values. We should be careful that our avoidance of separation does not result in too high a price—for our personal integrity and our common enterprises. If the emperor is not wearing any clothes, someone should report what he is seeing, even when that report is not expected. Sometimes an exit with voice, or a resignation with protest, can be a reform mechanism. At other times, a person simply owes it to himself to speak his mind while walking out the door.

5

The Institutionalized Person

When we speak about an "institutionalized person," we usually are referring to a prisoner or someone confined to a mental health institution. These are people whose actions and vision are restricted literally by the walls of an institution, their views of the world and their possible choices of behavior limited by the bricks-and-mortar boundaries of that setting. In a similar way, many of us have our vision and choices of action constrained by noncustodial institutions of which we are members. Institutionalized persons of this kind may not have their freedom of movement restricted by locked gates, but their view of the world and their actions are limited in a very real sense by the agenda of an institution that they have granted authority over their lives.

An institutionalized person has resolved, or avoided, the problem of conflicting agendas by simply accepting the institutional agenda. No problem exists because the personal agenda is identical to or subsumed under that of the institution. The expectations that form moral choice are the expectations of the corporate group, accepted and embraced as if they were one's own. Indeed, they have become one's own.

The model of the institutionalized person does not fit everyone whose actions conform to an institution's expectations. People may follow a group's agenda that conflicts with their personal reasons for a variety of reasons—financial rewards, avoidance of sanctions, protection of family interests. This kind of response will be discussed under the type of the "split personality." The institutionalized person is one who adheres to the corporate agenda because he has given the agenda-setting role to the institution. It is not a matter of following an agenda even though it conflicts with one's personal priorities, but of aligning one's personal priorities with the institutional agenda.

Eric Hoffer has described such a "true believer" as stripped of individual identity, assimilated into the collective body, as having no purpose, worth, or destiny apart from the group. "His only salvation is in rejecting his self and in finding a new life in the bosom of a holy corporate body—be it a church, a nation or a party."[1] We find people absorbed this way into a variety of institutions, with varying degrees of awareness and consent on the part of the individual.

The "Company Man"

The "company man" (it does seem that these people are most often men) is a familiar figure in our culture. He has dedicated himself to the company and has pledged his life to seeking its ends. The company has become the ultimate source of truth regarding behavior and beliefs, and its officers are the priests who mediate that truth. The company man response is not, of course, found only in the business world. Families, nation-states, churches, armies, street gangs, and political parties all contain company men who believe unquestioningly in the inherent morality of the group, ignoring the personal dimensions of their moral choices.

An expression of this type of response to institutional agendas hung in a store in rural Tennessee:

Remember This

If you work for a man, in heaven's name, work for him. If he pays you wages which supply your bread and butter, work for him. Speak well of him, stand by him, and stand by the institution he represents. If you are put in a pinch, an ounce of loyalty is worth a pound of cleverness. If you must vilify, condemn, and eternally disparage— resign your position, and when you are outside, damn to your heart's content. But as long as you are a part of the institution, do not condemn it. If you do that, you are losing the tendrils that are holding you to the institution, and at the first high wind that comes along, you will be uprooted and blown away and probably will never know the reason why.

Elbert Hubbard[2]

The institutionalized person adheres to what William Scott and David Hart have termed "the organizational imperative," which is the premise that "whatever is good for the individual can only come from the modern organization."[3] This premise justifies the extension of institutional control into all aspects of individuals' lives for their own good and calls for the modification of the values of all persons who affect the institution so that the institutional agenda is best served. One observer has termed this view the idea of the employee as "serf."[4]

Some company men intentionally act to sign on with the group; others are born into it. Just as individuals' bodies are physically committed to institutions both voluntarily and involuntarily, so both paths are followed in the confinement of personal agendas to the expectations of institutional settings. In many ways the alignment of personal and institutional agendas by chance rather than by choice is a simpler and less interesting phenomenon. Sometimes people readily follow an institutional lead because they have never been in a position to consider an alternative. Those institutions which have done the best job of socializing us from an early age are most likely to find willing subjects among their members. For example, for many men and women the traditional expectations of the institution of marriage have coincided with personal expectations because the partners have never been exposed to an alternative vision. Submissive wives and domineering husbands experience no conflict in agendas if that pattern of relationship is the only pattern they have ever known.

The church has often put forth its agenda in such an effective way over the course of members' lifetimes that a strong congruence exists between the agendas of adherents to the faith and those of the religious institution. "There is no salvation outside the church" is an effectively socializing message. The process of professional education can have this effect on students, as is evident in these excerpts from the journals of first-year law students who were being taught "to think like lawyers":

> [S]o much coming in, so few ways to comprehend it, that we do not "think" about it. We do it, over and over again, until it becomes automatic, like Pavlov's dog. In a situation like this we lose perspective on ourselves and we do not realize what others readily see. . . . Law School has simply become my life. Anything else seems trivial.

My attitude toward other people and issues has become one of indif-
ference. If it doesn't have anything to do with Law School, I don't
care about it.[5]

Patriotism has been the socializing force of one of our most
powerful institutions—the nation-state. Slogans quickly come to
mind which express and reinforce the view that personal and national agendas should coincide, not conflict: "My country, Right or
Wrong." "America, Love It or Leave It." "With God on Our Side."
Loyalty, of course, is the key. And loyalty is given freely, enthusi-
astically, and not after a process of critical appraisal of exactly what
the nation is expecting. Any conflict between a personal agenda
and a national agenda is seen as a call not to withhold allegiance to
the flag and all it stands for, but a call to get one's personal agenda
in order.

It appears that involuntary institutionalization of one's
agendas was much more common and much more easily accomplished in days past than at the end of the twentieth century.
Simple adoption of a single institution's expectations is most likely
in circumstances of social isolation, and we are all familiar with the
terms which describe the breakup of insular communities: mobility, urbanization, mass communications, pluralism, globalization.
Increasingly individuals are being exposed to new ideas, forced to
consider alternative views of the world and differing expectations
of how they should act. It is less likely today that someone will
unthinkingly fall into this pattern of behavior.

This social change does not signal the end of the company
man's response to corporate agendas. This change does mean that
making this response will more often be the result of deliberate
choice. The distinction between voluntary and involuntary institutionalization should be seen as points on the end of a continuum
rather than two rigid, exclusive options. In even the most isolated
circumstances, it is hard to imagine an individual growing to adult-
hood without encountering some glimmer of an alternative perspective, some pull to think that one's father or priest or president
should not always be followed. In like manner, as we proceed to
think about those who deliberately choose to align personal and
institutional agendas we should remember that their thoughts and
decisions are shaped by socialization processes that they may not
understand and that they certainly don't control.

Those who consciously decide to embrace a group's agenda as their own are choosing that group as their moral arbiter. The choice is to accept that set of expectations regardless of one's critical appraisal of their content which, in effect, means that there is no need to engage in such an assessment. The decision is to fashion one's life in accordance with the group agenda—without reflection or hesitation.

Why would an individual make such a decision? A partial answer can be found in the inclination to avoid the discomfort that accompanies making difficult moral choices.[6] Some persons find accepting responsibility for the morality of their choices to be a frightening burden and thus flee from the freedom of decision and action through membership in institutions that will direct their behavior.[7] They willingly renounce their own moral agency, accepting unquestioningly the judgments of the institution.

Apart from this basic psychological tendency, there are reasons individuals can give that support granting such moral authority to an institution. One reason could be an assessment that important interests would be served best through the efficiency that results from such a model. The power of a given enterprise to serve its function is often increased through the delivering of one's self to the endeavor. At a mundane level, I've discovered that squeezing in a tennis match before an important meeting or trying to play basketball while babysitting with a couple of children is a good way to undermine the recreational value of the activity. In such circumstances, the agendas of meetings or child care mix with the game's agenda with less satisfying results than if I had immersed myself in the game.

A better illustration of this phenomenon is the man in the Soviet Union who told a radio reporter in July of 1990 that he had believed everything the Communist party leaders had told him for thirty years. The man told this story as he was breaking out of the institution, submitting his resignation from the party. Such unswerving allegiance to an institution can be voluntarily given as people willfully surrender an independent perspective to reap the benefits being secured by that institution, benefits that accrue as a result of such unquestioned support. Over time, the cause being served by the institution can be forgotten with the institutional allegiance becoming an end in itself.

A second reason for submitting one's moral choices to an

institution is a matter of knowledge, a sense that the group's collective wisdom will tend to be more reliable than an individual's limited perspective. The institutions that are candidates for this kind of loyalty have a history of serving ideals that generates a confidence among their members that the group knows best. This is the spirit expressed in Bertolt Brecht's hymn to the Communist party:

> The individual has two
> The Party has a thousand eyes.
> The individual sees a city
> The Party sees seven states.
> The individual has his hour
> The Party has many hours.[8]

In a world in which each individual cannot have the capacity, energy, or time to decide each moral question at the outset, people understandably take direction from institutions.[9] This alternative is especially attractive in an increasingly complex world in which doing good requires more technical expertise and predicting results seems less possible.

Third, it could be argued that we have been looking at the question backwards, that the issue is often not why should a person follow an institutional agenda but why should a person *not* follow an institutional agenda. Michael Walzer gives us this description of a "morally serious" member of a group: "[H]e joins the group voluntarily, knowing what membership involves; he devotes time and energy to its inner life, sharing in the making of decisions; he acts publicly in its name or in the name of its ideals. Such a person—not any person—is obligated to act as he does, unless he is given good reasons why he ought not to do so."[10]

While this morally serious group member is not necessarily a company man, this description presents the case in a way that is supportive of the first two arguments. If institutions are to regulate our lives in a effective way, if the lessons of history and the wisdom of experience are to be brought meaningfully into the present, those institutions have to be able to count on their members. Institutions can succeed in approximating the ideals for which they were created only to the extent that loyal members support and advance their cause. Therefore, it could be argued, the presumption should be that we do suspend our individual judgment and follow institutional agendas.

An important phrase in Walzer's description, however, is, "unless he is given good reasons why he ought not to do so." This provision makes sense only if the individual is willing to listen to reasons to see if they are "good," a willingness that does not characterize a company man. Walzer's sense of a person's obligation to follow an institutional agenda is that it is a prima facie obligation, that is, an obligation which has force if, and only if, there are not conflicting obligations which outweigh that particular obligation.

While there may be appropriate times and places for us to institutionalize our moral judgment, a long history of moral philosophizing—accented by our experience with nazism—argues that "just following orders" is not a response to institutional agendas that should rule our lives. Signing up with a few groups—a company, a church, a political party—and then suspending our own moral judgment seems instinctively inappropriate on some level. Henry David Thoreau, never at a loss for a stinging comment, characterized soldiers who appeared to have taken this option as mere shadows or reminiscences of humanity: "In most cases there is no free exercise whatever of the judgment or moral sense; but they put themselves on a level with wood and earth and stones. . . . Such command no more respect than men of straw or a lump of dirt. They have the same sort of worth only as horses and dogs."[11]

There is also a paradox in the company man model that I think goes a long way toward explaining its continuing appeal. While many of us may resist this type of response in our own lives, for example in our employment setting, we want company men working for us. I recall a series of television advertisements about the "Bache Broker." These spots pictured the Bache Broker riding on the commuter train in the morning, alone, before daylight; and the Bache Broker getting up from dinner conversation to make a call to see how financial markets were doing on the other side of the world. In short, the Bache Broker was always on call, if not at work, devoting every segment of his life to getting an investment edge. I had two reactions to the advertisements: (1) I never wanted to be a Bache Broker; (2) if I ever had any money to invest, I would probably want someone like a Bache Broker working for me.

A friend and I were discussing an interesting book written by Rand and Dana Crowley Jack about an increasing reluctance among attorneys to fit into a "hired gun" mold.[12] My friend had quit the practice of law precisely because he could no longer balance his personal agenda with the professional expectations that he engage in partisan advocacy for a client, no matter how he evaluated the consequences of that advocacy in terms of justice. He was quick to acknowledge, however, that if he ever had to choose an attorney to defend any of his children, he would want a hired gun, he would want an advocate who would pursue any avenue that would benefit his child.

What would the company man's response look like for our friend John, a believer in equality of persons, who belongs to an exclusive country club? If John fits the company man profile, he resolves the potential conflict by accepting as authoritative the club's "party line." The first possibility is that John would never have faced such a quandary. Socialized into a family and community in which the club is a way of life, John may well have continued in his club membership without ever raising the question. It may never occur to him that an inconsistency exists.

It is also possible, however, that John will be brought face-to-face with the potential conflict. Perhaps through the challenges of others or a self-exploration of the meaning of his personal commitment to equal treatment for all persons, John could come to ask whether a conflict exists that must be resolved. If his response is that of the company man, he will readily embrace the institution's view on the issue and consider the matter closed. An institutionalized John would simply accept the new agenda, abandoning his old ideas about equal treatment. This acceptance is not the result of a careful consideration of the issues involved; that type of response belongs to "the convert," as described in chapter 9. The response of the institutionalized person is an automatic deferral to the institution's view.

Knowing that complex, difficult issues may be involved, John could be grateful for having these matters cleared up by others who have had more experience with them and have spent more time reflecting on them. He can continue his club membership with a clear conscience, relieved that what might have been a conflict in agendas turns out not to be a conflict after all.

The Victim

Not all institutionalized persons accept institutional boundaries as willingly as the company man. A second type is that of the "victim." Victims do not embrace institutional confinement but rage against it. They do not choose to submit to the power of others but feel trapped by it. Theirs is not a response which resolves moral conflict but which dramatizes the distance between belief and action.

The victim's response is almost a nonresponse. The other responses to conflicts between personal and institutional agendas that are described in this book have a voluntary element to them. The victim's response is, "I don't have any choice." While the company man submits to an institutional agenda that defines his personal agenda, the victim submits to an institutional agenda that is at odds with personal values. The contrary personal agenda still exists, but this person has not been able to act upon it.

This type of response is evident in the feelings and actions of many battered women. A large number of battered women continue in a relationship with, indeed continue to live with, the men who are abusing them. The obvious question that comes to an observer is, "Why doesn't she get out?" Lenore Walker describes the "learned helplessness" that accounts for this kind of continuing victimization.[13] This condition is based in a belief that one has little or no control over her life. She expects that her response to a situation will not be effective in producing a better outcome, but this expectation does not have to be an accurate one. If a person does have control over response-outcome variables but does not believe she does, she will still respond with learned helplessness. Such people give up when they believe the situation is hopeless. Eventually, "once the [battered] women are operating from a belief of helplessness, the perception becomes reality and they become passive, submissive, 'helpless.'"[14] Repeated battering has a debilitating effect on problem-solving abilities, as women become blind to their options and perceive an increasingly narrow range of responses. Learned helplessness can be learned during childhood from experiences of lack of control and inability to affect outcomes, especially for girls whose socialization has stressed passivity and dependency.[15] Repeated battering diminishes the motivation to respond and damages the cognitive ability to perceive success. One's emotional well-being suffers as one becomes depressed, developing severely pessimistic beliefs about the efficacy of acting. In one study, the initial emotional responses to battering were anger or hatred. "Eventually, however, these emotions gave way to feelings of hopelessness and despair, with many such women describing themselves as 'zombies.'"[16]

The core of the victim's response is the feeling of being trapped, the hopelessness that comes with the sense that one is in an intolerable situation for which there's no escape. Battered women are an extreme example of this response, but there are others. Financial dependency can elicit a victim's response, as testified to by Tennessee Ernie Ford when he sang about a life so hopeless that it was beyond the reach of divine intervention: "St. Peter don't you call me cause I can't go; I owe my soul to the company store."[17] The coercion of a master's whip, a police officer's pistol, a priest's sacrament, or a parent's belt can lead people to adhere to institutional agendas that differ dramatically from their own.

John's response to country club practices that contradict his personal values could be that of the victim. (In drawing this parallel, I do not mean to suggest in any way that the victimization of someone like our hypothetical character remotely compares to the oppression and suffering of abused women and children.) John may have been subject to a domineering family for so long that he has given up on acting on any impulses that are contrary to his parents. He may be so dependent on peer acceptance or so reliant on being judged a success within that subculture that he cannot choose unacceptable courses of action. His identity may be so enmeshed in the social fabric surrounding the club that he cannot imagine that he could confront the system and still be himself.

In such circumstances, John would simply capitulate. This acquiescence is a form of victimization when John believes his compliance violates his personal agenda. He knows he should do otherwise; he wishes he could do otherwise. But he can't. He has not resolved the tension between the agendas the way the company man has. He has simply been unable to bring himself to act. The strength and courage that are required to go against the stream are beyond his reach. John suffers because of his incapacity, but he suffers in silence.

When we have been brutalized by an institutional agenda, there is a difference between responding as a victim and as a survivor. Dictionary definitions clarify the distinction: A victim suffers from a destructive or injurious action, such as the victim of an automobile accident; a survivor has endured or lived through an affliction or adversity. *Persist* and *succeed* are listed among the synonyms for *survive*.

The victim has suffered a loss of personal center or power. His personal agenda has been rendered ineffectual, if not destroyed. The institution controls his life; personal responsibility becomes an illusory concept. The survivor is one who thinks: I have been powerless but now I have some power to figure out how to respond to this adversity. The survivor is not willing to allow himself to be enslaved by the agendas of others. There remains a personal core with a power to choose, and the choice will be one of the other types of responses described in this book.

We all surrender bits and pieces of our lives to institutional structures. We know that some corporate structures are necessary. We don't function in isolation from groups; we can't function without some of the order provided by institutional agendas. In practice, we all operate out of a taken-for-grantedness that parallels to some degree the institutionalized person style. So the question is not necessarily whether, but how much? How often? How far? And how do we go about answering these questions?

We must be wary of temptations to surrender too much of our lives to any institution. A responsible person, as described in chapter 2, has an obligation to respond in light of her critical interpretation of what's going on in the world, accepting accountability for anticipated responses to her choices. A wholesale surrender of choice to others, the reduction of one's self to a moral automaton, violates this notion of what it means to be a free moral agent. Our legal tradition refuses to allow a person to sell himself into slavery. Our moral tradition should do no less.

6

The Split Personality

One response to the conflict between personal agendas and institutional agendas is to divide the world into separate parts. Institutional agendas are supreme in the realm appropriate for those particular institutions, while one's personal or private life is maintained as the reserve to be ruled by the personal agenda. In this compartmentalization of one's world, conflicting personal agendas and institutional agendas exist side by side, with each set of expectations being dominant in the proper arena. In effect, the struggle becomes one not of determining which set of expectations is correct, but of determining the boundaries that divide one's life.

This is the approach taken by many commentators on professional ethics and is common in areas of human endeavor that lie far outside the professions. In one's public or institutional life, the agendas of public and corporate groups are accepted as authoritative. An employee knows and follows the company's agenda; a private knows and follows the orders that come down through the military hierarchy; an attorney knows and follows the profession's code of professional responsibility. These agendas are followed as long as the expectations of one's public roles do not inappropriately intrude into the realm of the private and personal.

This approach is not one in which, in the moment of decision, the claims of the personal and the institutional agendas are compared and weighed and a choice is made to follow the institutional agenda. Rather, this response is one of granting authority, before the fact, to the institutional agenda within a specified realm. Distinctive demands are placed on politicians, doctors, truck drivers, pro-life leaders, mothers receiving AFDC (Aid to Families with Dependent Children), waiters, Greenpeace activists. The culture of each of these settings establishes expectations that are accepted as legitimate, even if those expectations might not bear up under the scrutiny of "ordinary morality" outside these peculiar circumstances.

The rules-of-the-game model discussed in chapter 3 is a good illustration of this kind reasoning. It stipulates two (or more) distinct, even conflicting, codes of conduct that are valid in their separate arenas. A corporate executive who devotes time and energy to any responsibilities other than making as much money as possible for the owners of the business is seen as acting as a "principal," a private party, rather than an "agent" of the business.[1] Therefore, such actions do not fit the corporate agenda, and any use of company resources in such pursuits is improper, even irresponsible. The same activity could be viewed as proper if the person is acting on her own, as an individual rather than a representative of the corporation.

Those who adopt the most rigid rules-of-the-game approach claim a certain immunity from any moral criticism that has its roots outside of the game. When a "split personality" confronts accusations based on ethical principles that are external to the institution, a consistent response is, "I was just obeying the rules"—a more general variation of, "I was just following orders." The model of the split personality is similar to the "institutionalized person," in that the immediate response to institutional agendas is to follow them, at least within the acknowledged realm of the institution. The crucial difference, however, is that the split personality adheres to an institutional agenda in spite of moral convictions to the contrary, not because the institutional agenda has been granted the authority to determine what one's moral convictions should be. As a result, persons who adopt the mode of split personality often feel coerced in their actions, making choices that seem barely to be choices at all. Indeed, some observers feel that the public actions of most persons are their own only in a significantly restricted sense, and that to insist that persons can choose in ways contrary to institutional expectations is to focus on the formalities of the situation rather than on its center.[2]

Herman Melville has given us a classic account of this kind of conflict in his story of *Billy Budd*. Billy Budd was an exemplary sailor in the British navy. Following two mutinies in the British fleet, Billy was falsely charged with mutinous intent by Master-at-

Arms Claggart—an officer who was drawn as the epitome of evil as Billy was of innocence. Captain Starry Vere summoned Billy to his cabin where Claggart made the charge directly. Shocked by the charge and suffering from a speech defect, Billy was unable to utter any words in his defense. Repeated efforts by Captain Vere to elicit a response from Billy were unsuccessful and, indeed, only deepened his plight. Finally Billy's arm shot out and felled Claggart with a single fatal blow. At his court-martial Billy testified that he bore no malice against Claggart. "Could I have used my tongue I would not have struck him. But he foully lied to my face and in presence of my captain, and I had to say something, and I could only say it with a blow, God help me!"[3]

At Billy Budd's court-martial Captain Vere attempts to convince the hearing officers to accept the approach of a split personality. Vere's chosen task is to convince the officers that they should sentence to death a person acknowledged to be "innocent before God." His appeal is that they should set aside personal convictions and follow the agendas of the institutions of which they are members: "In receiving our commissions we in the most important regard ceased to be natural free-agents. Do these buttons that we wear attest that our allegiance is to Nature? No. To the King. Our vowed responsibility is this: That however pitilessly that law may operate, we nevertheless adhere to it and administer it."[4] Decisions such as the one being urged by Captain Vere are often the result of calculations that a course of action is the lesser of two evils, or that complying with a single agenda item in one instance is justifiable only because of broader or longer term benefits that flow from institutional loyalty. In Billy Budd's court-martial, the values of respect for the law and military discipline were seen as broader goods that outweighed just treatment of this single person.

A similar kind of conflict arose for a senior administrator at Vanderbilt University when that university found itself in the position of hosting a regional Davis Cup tennis match. As teams had been eliminated through the earlier rounds, the regional contest matched the teams of the United States and the Union of South Africa. Many persons on campus felt that the university was presented with an opportunity to make a statement against apartheid and that the offer to host the match should be withdrawn. Once it was clear that the university was firm in its resolve that political or ideological tests should not be used to judge who should be permitted on campus, this senior administrator and others faced a conflict.

She was unalterably opposed to apartheid and to the ideals for which the South African government stood. Her personal moral convictions would have led her to oppose holding the tennis match on campus and to protest the event as vigorously as possible if the match were held. By virtue of her position in the university hierarchy, however, it appeared that she had two options: to act in accord with the institution's agenda or to surrender her position. The fact that she did not resign was no indication of lack of commitment to the ideals of equality or the depth of her feeling of revulsion over the political climate in South Africa. It appeared that in this instance she was virtually being forced to take the option of the split personality. Without acknowledging the moral legitimacy of the university's agenda she nonetheless accepted it, apparently judging that more benefit (benefit as judged by her personal agenda) could come from her continuing in her position than from resigning.

Max Weber has given us a classic example of differentiating moral responses according to the position from which one acts. He divides public officials into two ideal types, politicians and administrative officials. Following her proper vocation, the genuine official will not engage in politics but in impartial administration: "It is in the nature of officials of high moral standing . . . to be irresponsible politicians."[5] Similarly the conduct of politicians is subject to exactly the opposite principle of responsibility from that of the civil servant.

Following this model, the civil servant will, and should, act in ways that would be irresponsible outside of her place in the bureaucracy. She is not to concern herself with the consequences of her official actions but is to obey orders as if they agreed with her own convictions. Weber is not suggesting that all citizens should act this way—indeed, the proper task of the politician is precisely the opposite. He is suggesting that the administrative official compartmentalize her life and in her official capacity act in ways that would be irresponsible and irrational outside of that compartment.

There are two important differences between the institutionalized person and the split personality. The first difference is the constant recognition of the distinction between the group's agenda and the personal agenda. If the advertising world caught the essence of the institutionalized person in the Bache Broker, those who market products also gave popular voice to the split personality type with such slogans as "AMF Makes Weekends," "It's Miller Time," and "The Night Belongs to Michelob." The reality captured by the commercials pushing these products is that many of us spend much of our time doing things we really don't want to do, or at least that we wouldn't choose to do if we were in control of all of our life's circumstances. Many people go to work and follow the company's agenda during the hours that they have given to the company. Personal choice is more fully realized when the clock strikes five o'clock, when they escape through the factory gates and move into the world that is more closely ordered to their personal agendas.

The true workaholic is an institutionalized person not a split personality. There may be employees who work as many hours or who follow company expectations as slavishly as the workaholic. But the workaholic is the one who meets those expectations because he wants to. The fulfillment and satisfaction of giving one's life over to the corporation can come only when one's personal agenda has been aligned with those corporate expectations. The split personality surrenders large portions of his life to the corporation with the continuous recognition that this is really not what he would choose to do if he were freer from certain external constraints. The split personality not only is pressured, but feels pressured to conform. The experience is one of not being free, and the acts performed in conforming with the group's expectations are perceived as nonvoluntary actions.[6] The label of institutionalized person, on the other hand, fits better the descriptions of how private persons seem to disappear in the organization when they take on public roles. In this view, the individual cannot be considered to be herself when fulfilling the demands of representing the group.[7]

Karl Marx captured this aspect of modern life in his notion of the alienated worker.[8] In a broad sense, someone is alienated from an institution when, given her situation, she would normally be expected to have a sense of loyalty toward that institution but in fact does not.[9] As noted earlier, while the literature on professional ethics seems to give support for this type of approach to conflicting agendas, this response is not restricted to the professions. In fact, it may well be that persons in professional positions, who often have had more career choices, may tend to be less likely than others to be alienated from their vocational pursuits.

The institutionalized person tends to see institutions as positive agencies through which we can promote the common good. The liberal notion of the welfare state that promotes our shared moral values and embodies a vision of the kind of society we desire fits this view. For the split personality, institutions are necessary restraining forces, agencies we support because of the undesirable consequences that would flow from their absence or ineffectiveness. The concept of the watchdog state is a view of the state more in tune with the view that we do not commit ourselves to an institution, but only grudgingly give our assent because of the need to use the institution for other purposes.

The pressure to follow institutional agendas that conflict with personal agendas should not be underestimated. The self-preservation instinct that exists in societies and organizations produces a coercion to conform, to be loyal to the group. These pressures provide an incentive for members to find a way to justify adherence to the institution's expectations, even when such adherence is in significant ways contrary to one's personal values. Sissela Bok has observed that the emphasis on competition and achieving material success that so marks our society also generates intense pressures to cut moral corners.[10] Preoccupation with concerns such as winning elections and outselling competitors lead many to participate in a duplicity that they might otherwise resist. These same pressures and concerns lead people to cooperate with institutional practices which they find objectionable. The split personality is mindful of the contrary demands of her personal morality. But, as much research has shown, individuals will act contrary to their personal ethical judgments when faced with negative consequences from external sources.[11] And institutions are powerfully able to inflict negative sanctions on those who do not conform to group expectations.

The first difference, then, between the split personality and the institutionalized person is that the former does not surrender moral authority to the institution. She may choose to do the group's bidding in certain instances, but she does not necessarily like it. The second difference, related to the first, is the maintenance of a critical principle to check the reach of institutional agendas. The nurturing of a healthy, vibrant personal agenda means that an independent source of judgment exists to determine when a group's expectations have intruded too far into one's personal life.

The most important decisions for the split personality may be those which determine how much of one's world is to be governed by personal agendas and how much is to be given over to various, often competing, institutions. The admonition to "render unto Caesar the things that are Caesar's, and unto God the things that are God's" doesn't tell us much until we know which things are Caesar's and which are God's. In light of the problem of personal morality in institutional settings, we could summarize the central concern of the split personality thus: Render unto the company, the family, the church (as examples) the things that are theirs, but not the things that are mine!

Deciding which parts of one's life are subject to personal agendas and which are subject to institutional agendas is related, in practice, to the perceived size of the gap between one's personal morality and the group's expectations. Almost inevitably the range deemed appropriate for an institution's agenda decreases as the discrepancy between what the group thinks is right and what the individual thinks is right increases. For this reason, the splitting of the world into disparate parts is not as easy a resolution of the conflicting agendas problem as it first appears. The boundaries are never settled. The movement among adjoining moral spheres could be thought of as a random continental drift, with the moral equivalent of earthquakes occurring as one plate collides with another.

The approach of the split personality may be a fairly common one for people like John in our hypothetical situation. Treating people equally, regardless of race or gender, is an item on John's agenda. He expects to act fairly in making decisions that affect others but finds himself in an institution that carries a different set of expectations. His choice of the response of the split personality will not allow John to resolve the conflict, but it may provide him with a way to live with it.

Membership in the exclusionary club conflicts with John's egalitarian beliefs. He cannot bring himself to embrace the club's philosophy and thereby rid himself of the tension, but he can contain it. He could determine that the sphere of the exclusive country club is a fairly narrow, easily confined area of his life. His club membership does not prohibit him from engaging in progressive politics, from practicing affirmative action in the workplace, from teaching his children nondiscriminatory principles. John's decision is to create this one compartment in his life in which he will allow institutional expectations to violate this feature of his personal agenda. John's membership in this group obligates him to do different things than he would do absent this membership. Unwilling or unable to free himself from these external constraints by resigning, he somewhat reluctantly conforms to the club's expectations, but only in this specified area. He pays his dues, follows the rules, and pursues the full meaning of equal treatment of persons in the rest of his life's activities.

The split personality, in given contexts, is content just to follow institutional agendas. One problem with this narrow focus is that it excludes consideration of the fact that many individuals find ways to incorporate their personal values into their responses to institutional agendas. And group memberships can almost always be terminated in one way or another. The next question can always be asked: "Why were those the rules that you thought you should obey?" Critics of this model lament a culture that fosters conformity rather than conviction, group loyalty rather than individual accountability, and, picking up on the game language, despair that a person is evaluated more for his willingness to "play ball" than for his morals.[12]

The response of the split personality is seen by some observers as an attempt to bring unrealistic simplification to a complex world. Gerald Postema argues that rules and codes that fit within certain compartments are not adequate for addressing contemporary institutional moral dilemmas. What is called for is a sense of responsibility and sound practical judgment that depend, in part, on "one's ability to draw on the resources of a broader moral experience. This, in turn, requires that one seek to achieve a fully integrated moral personality."[13] This strategy for maintaining professional and personal integrity is at odds with the compartmentalization inherent in the split personality approach.

The split personality response may be less satisfying for many people than either of the purer types of the hermit or the institutionalized person. From one end of the spectrum, the compartmentalizing response can be seen to be too great an abdication of moral responsibility. Individuals are following group agendas while acknowledging their inadequacies, even their immorality. In the workplace, the profit motive may reign supreme; in the political party, the party boss may go unchallenged; in the government, unfair practices may go on without protest.

From the other end of the spectrum, this response can be seen as providing too little support for institutions, undercutting their efforts to make their needed civilizing contributions. At no time does the split personality grant to institutions a moral authority that overrides the personal preferences of the multitude of individuals who interact with them. The possibility continues to exist that the individual will decide that the institution has crossed the boundary that protects the personal sphere. Group effectiveness therefore is always threatened by the potential of individual choices to balk, even revolt. Thus, this response can be judged to be either too compliant or too resistant in the face of institutional expectations.

As a result, escape from this type of response to one of the others is more likely than for either the hermit or the institutionalized person. The split personality maintains multiple centers of moral authority. While each of these centers supposedly is supreme within its own realm, there continues to be a moral center that is personal, one that is acknowledged to be closer to the individual, more fully an expression of the self's autonomous moral judgment. Following institutional agendas is always done with an awareness that the personal agenda may be different. From time to time that difference will become great enough that the authority granted to a corporate agenda will have to be withdrawn. The monitoring of the size of those differences, as well as the location of the boundaries between the distinct realms, results in split personalities that are often unstable personalities.

7

The Reformer

On August 28, 1963, Martin Luther King, Jr., spoke these words in front of the Lincoln Memorial:

We cannot turn back. There are those who are asking the devotees of civil rights, "When will you be satisfied?" We can never be satisfied as long as the Negro is the victim of the unspeakable horrors of police brutality. We can never be satisfied as long as our bodies, heavy with the fatigue of travel, cannot gain lodging in the motels of the highways and the hotels of the cities. We cannot be satisfied as long as the Negro's basic mobility is from a smaller ghetto to a larger one. We can never be satisfied as long as a Negro in Mississippi cannot vote and a Negro in New York believes he has nothing for which to vote. No, no we are not satisfied, and we will not be satisfied until justice rolls down like waters and righteousness like a mighty stream.[1]

The "reformer," dissatisfied with institutional agendas that contradict his personal agenda, has a dream and is not content to live in the midst of social expectations that deny that dream.

This approach to dealing with the conflict between an institutional agenda and one's personal agenda leads to attempts to change the institutional agenda. Unwilling to abandon the institution as does the "hermit," unwilling to surrender one's moral autonomy as does the "institutionalized person," and unwilling to set one's morality to the side from time to time as does the "split personality," the reformer seeks to resolve the conflict by bringing the group's expectations in line with his personal values.

The reformer sees our societal institutions as subject to

more control than do many of us. An example of this attitude can be seen in Kenneth Howard's response to Michael Walzer's classic essay, "Political Action: The Problem of Dirty Hands."[2] Walzer argues that the dilemma of dirty hands, the problem of doing what is right and yet being guilty of a moral wrong, is a central feature of political life. People do not succeed in politics without getting their hands dirty, without using means that are morally undesirable. One of Walzer's examples illustrates his point. He describes a candidate who is a moral person, who has principles and a history of adherence to those principles that lead us to support him. In order to win the election, the candidate must make a deal with a dishonest ward boss involving the granting of school construction contracts. The candidate is extremely reluctant to consider the deal. Because he has scruples of this sort, according to Walzer, we hope he will overcome his scruples and make the deal. "We know he is doing right when he makes the deal because he knows he is doing wrong."[3] We will return to Walzer's views when we discuss the "accommodator" in chapter 8; it is Howard's response to this "dirty hands" problem that bears on the typical response of the reformer.

Howard's approach to conflicting agendas in the political realm is summed up this way: "Politics is not how you find it but what you make it." He thinks Walzer's problem is that he views politics as something external to us, as a system into which we are fed. If dirty hands are an inevitable part of politics, it is because we have let political institutions get away from us. "What is objectionable about Walzer is his apparent acceptance of this fact. I have argued that there is no reason we cannot change things if we want to."[4]

We can change things if we want to—this is the attitude of the reformer. And if there is no reason why the agendas of our vast political institutions cannot be changed, surely the expectations of other social institutions can be altered as well. The reformer's call is to recognize that social expectations have been created by people and that they can be changed by people. If the institutional agenda conflicts with the personal agenda, change the institutional agenda.

Several tactical routes are available to the person who is not content to live with the institutional status quo. One approach to bringing about a convergence of social and personal agendas seems to assume the existence of a moral invisible hand which brings institutional success to those who are moral. For example, the split personality is convinced that corporate expectations can be met only by distinguishing one's choices in the social role from one's personal morality. As we understood this approach in chapter 6, success in the business world (or the political world or certain social circles) comes from following a set of rules distinct from those which ordinarily govern moral choice. One type of reformer believes such distinctions are misguided, preferring instead a moral code such as the following: "We believe that a strong code of morality in any business is the first step toward its success. We believe that ethical managers are winning managers."[5] If one sticks by her personal agenda, institutional success will follow. If such an approach works in business, it seems that such an approach would apply to a variety of the other social roles that we assume. It appears that it would also be true that ethical police officers are successful police officers, that ethical diplomats are successful diplomats, that ethical investigative reporters and political campaign managers and labor organizers are successful.

Of course, one difficulty is to determine what "ethical" and "successful" mean in this context. If being ethical means that a person operates in social settings in accord with the norms that comprise his or her personal agenda, and being successful is a measure of the extent to which one meets institutional expectations, then this type of reformer approaches the problem from the opposite direction from the institutionalized person. The problem of conflicting agendas is solved not by changing the individual's morality to match the group's, but by steadfastly sticking to one's personal agenda in the confidence that satisfaction of institutional expectations will follow.

Steering such a course obviously requires a great deal of inner-directedness and personal strength. Even so, this approach may well be minimizing the extent of the conflict between the two types of agendas and thus faces at least two dangers. The reformer who assumes the possibility of easily forging a compatibility between personal morality and social expectations runs the risk of being marginalized in the direction of the hermit or being co-opted into the role of the institutionalized person.

Considering the first risk, a person who takes institutional expectations less seriously can more easily conduct himself without reference to, or at least with less deference to, group agendas. The fact that this individual does not accept social norms as authoritative, however, does not necessarily mean that other members of the group will not enforce those norms. A variety of institutional responses may apply to members who place their own agenda above that of the group: forced resignation, excommunication, court-martial, shunning, impeachment, recall, divorce, disbarment, revocation of license, disinheritance, expulsion, exile, banishment, and the ultimate sanction, execution. The too-easy assumption that one can follow personal norms in the face of contrary institutional agendas may result not in the reform of the institution but in the exit of the individual, transforming the reformer into a hermit.

Even if the individual is not formally removed from the group, he may cease to be a functioning member. This person may be tolerated as harmless and simply moved to the margin of the group's life. Knowing smiles and winks of the eye become the routine response to the dreamers, the idealists who don't take enough account of the social realities that others believe should inform the choices of the group's members. Rather than producing institutional reform through their strength of character, these would-be crusaders pass into a quixotic tradition of tilting at windmills.

A second risk exists for those who counsel, "Be ethical and you will be successful." In actual practice, the temptation is to define what is ethical in terms of what brings success. Just such a reversal is identified by Max Weber as he described the meaning the concept of "the calling" had for many post-Reformation Protestants: the only way of living acceptably was "through the fulfillment of the obligations imposed upon the individual by his position in the world."[6] One's moral obligation was to fulfill his duties in worldly affairs, and it was all too easy to view success in that arena as a sign of moral uprightness.

The task of defining what is moral is difficult, with the answers often being amorphous or unclear. The task of defining success is usually much easier: winning an election, earning a large salary, receiving community awards, making high grades, winning cases, etc. If one assumes a natural convergence between being ethical and succeeding, it would not be surprising to find clear evidence of the latter being interpreted as signs of the former. In essence, conforming to institutional expectations becomes the content of the personal agenda, and the reformer becomes an institutionalized person.

However, most reformers do not attempt to minimize conflict by equating morality with institutional success. The conflict between personal and institutional norms is clear for them, and any effort to bring about change is expected to be a struggle. These crusaders share certain traits—questioning established interpretations, bridling under unthinking conformity, resisting conventional values or patterns—but may take different paths toward institutional reform. We will look at three examples here, arrayed along a continuum from moderate to radical: working within channels, whistle blowing, and resigning under protest.

Most institutions have acceptable channels for reforming practices or policies. The variety and effectiveness of such avenues will be less in autocratic organizations than in democratic groups, and in hierarchical settings those at the top have more options than those at the bottom. But some mechanism for legitimate change usually exists. A reformer can engage in fairly modest efforts to alter institutional agendas by making use of these opportunities: raising personal concerns at designated meetings, sending memos to appropriate people within the organization, discretely sending up trial balloons. Sometimes, of course, institutions only appear to be open to change, but actually are not. The "suggestion box" that serves as little more than a wastebasket can be found in such organizations. But if the distance between personal agenda and institutional agenda is not too great, and the institution is responsive to the expressions of discontent, the reforming activity may be effective at this level.

A second, more aggressive, option for the crusading spirit can be characterized under the general heading of whistle blowing. The whistle blower dissents from the institution's agenda, as does the reformer who works through channels. The difference is that the whistle blower adds the elements of breach of loyalty and accusation to her chosen form of action.[7] Whistle blowing involves stepping out of channels to speak against policies or practices of the group. Such public accusations of misconduct are invariably seen as disloyal as the "insider"—the family member, the line officer, the party member—takes her case beyond the group. Whistle blowing is based on the kind of sentiment expressed in the 1974 code adopted by the Engineers Council for Professional Development: "Engineers shall hold paramount the safety, health and welfare of the public in the performance of their professional duties. . . . Engineers shall not approve nor seal plans and/or specifications that are not of a design safe to the public health and welfare."[8]

One observer sees this encouragement of engineers to act on their own assessment of the public good to be "sufficient to destroy the degree of coordination essential to the effective functioning of modern bureaucracies."[9] The statement by General Motors Board Chairman James M. Roche, made in response to Ralph Nader's encouragement of whistle blowing, is not an atypical corporate response: "Some of the enemies of business now encourage an employee to be disloyal to the enterprise. They want to create suspicion and disharmony and pry into the proprietary interests of the business. However this is labelled—industrial espionage, whistle blowing or professional responsibility—it is another tactic for spreading disunity and creating conflict."[10] Whistle blowers focus on a different problem: "The real ethical problem threatening society in this area is the preponderance of public (and private) employees who will studiously ignore crimes going on about them in order to protect their paychecks, their advancement and their peer support."[11]

Whistle blowers have often been previously frustrated in their attempts to bring about change through "legitimate" means and feel that the more aggressive conduct is justified. The story of Eastern Airlines pilot Dan Gellert illustrates the path that can lead a loyal employee to become a whistle blower and a adversary within his institution.[12] On December 29, 1972, an Eastern Airlines L-1011 flying from New York to Miami crashed eighteen miles from Miami's International Airport, killing ninety-three passengers and five crew members. Gellert had previously filed a verbal report about the inadvertent disengagement of the autopilot on a L-1011 he had been flying, an occurrence similar to a training incident that had also been reported. Suspecting the autopilot problem might have contributed to the Miami accident and having received no word of action following his first report, he sent a two-page memorandum to the board chairman and the president and vice-president of operations.

After he received a reply from Frank Borman, vice-president of operations, that it was doubtful that any one problem caused the accident, Gellert sent copies of the memo to the Airline Pilots Association and the National Transportation Safety Board (NTSB), which was about to hold hearings on the crash. Gellert was called to testify at the hearings and, following the board's release of its findings, Eastern decided to modify the autopilot design. Five months later Gellert twice experienced the same problem and again wrote to the NTSB.

In the years that followed, Gellert at various times found himself demoted, grounded, and suspended. Each time he filed a grievance that was brought before the Eastern Airlines Pilots System Board of Adjustment, which had the power to settle such disputes. Each time the board ruled in favor of Gellert. After winning the multiple grievance hearings, Gellert resorted to the legal system filing a lawsuit against Eastern charging "civil conspiracy to force me out of employment."[13]

This journey from an internal memorandum to a lawsuit is an example of a group member going outside of channels when he believed the system was not being responsive to his reforming efforts. This story also demonstrates the kind of institutional response a whistle blower, or anyone adopting more aggressive reform tactics, may encounter. A reformer who contemplates "going public" with problems should not underestimate the institutional interest in keeping such discussions "in house." The lot of a whistle blower often is not a happy one. Groups demand solidarity, and the social disapproval of "tattling" survives childhood in many quarters.

Among the weapons of retaliation available to an institution, weapons that can exact large career and emotional costs and devastate family life, are blacklisting, transfer, and personal harassment.[14] These forms of retaliation are most directly associated with the workplace, but parallel strategies exist in other arenas. Blacklisting prevents a dismissed employee from finding comparable employment as institutional leaders agree to warn each other of potential troublemakers. Whistle blowers who resign in protest or who are fired following their public activities often find that their professional careers have been destroyed. In other cases, the dissenter is not fired but demoted or transferred, given positions far from home or with nothing to do. Assignment to tasks outside of one's area of expertise or well below one's level of competence may be the first step in a process leading to dismissal or forced resignation.

Personal forms of retaliation are also directed at whistle blowers. Billie Garde complained about a superior's use of his office for his private political aggrandizement and to exploit others sexually. Her superior fired her and subsequently sought and secured a judicial order taking away custody of her children from her.[15] Sexual harassment of female whistle blowers has been widely reported. The movie *Silkwood* dramatized the story of Karen Silkwood, whose car mysteriously ran off the road while she was apparently taking information about her employer to a reporter. When responses can range from character assassination to ruined careers to physical violence and death threats,[16] decisions to blow the whistle should not be made lightly.

Albert Hirschman has labeled these kinds of reform tactics—whether working in channels or whistle blowing—as "voice," speaking up in an effort to change the practices, policies, or outputs of an institution. He distinguishes this option from that of "exit" (the hermit's choice), noting that while withdrawing from a group requires a clear-cut either/or decision, voice is an "art," the practice of which continually evolves in new directions. The greater one's loyalty to an institution, the greater the probability that she will choose voice over exit. And while an easy exit makes voice less likely, the possibility of a member's exit may well strengthen the effectiveness of her use of voice as a reforming tactic.[17] A dissenter who is not willing to quit or at least to take the more aggressive course of the whistle blower, may be seen as an easy target for domestication, thereby negating her hope that she could work more effectively from inside the group.

A third option for reform is resignation under protest. While whistle blowers often wish to remain a part of the institution, a more extreme response to an intolerable divergence between group and personal agendas is to get out. Leaving becomes more than the act of a hermit when the exit is part of a visible protest so that the action may yet lead to some alteration of institutional policies or practices. Whether through press conferences, letters, lawsuits, or just speaking one's mind publicly before slamming the door, this reformer hopes to change the institution even as his membership is (at least temporarily) terminated.

This approach combines Hirschman's "exit" and "voice" options. Exit with voice is often the last resort for a loyal group member who finds an institutional expectation to be intolerable.

Loyal members, especially influential members, will hesitate to exit for fear that the organization may go from bad to worse if they leave.[18] Even if they continue to care about improving the institution, at some point they may determine that resigning in protest over the group's agenda holds the promise of being a more effective option than continuing to fight from within. It is the fact that they do still care, that they do still feel a certain loyalty to the institution, that will cause them to speak their words of protest and reform as they exit, rather than simply separating themselves from the group. When holding expectations for the institution that exceed its accomplishments, a person may voice criticism while withdrawing for the benefit of the group. This kind of reformer does retain a certain loyalty to the corporate body. On the other hand, simple withdrawal can be disloyal, depriving the institution of an opportunity to respond positively to constructive criticism.

Effective reform efforts are almost always group efforts. One's choice of the reformer's response will often depend on the possibility of alliances with others, the formation of subgroups or enclaves within institutions in pursuit of a common cause. Such action takes place not in isolation but with others, through mutual discovery and support. This communal dimension, present in most responses, is especially important to the reformer. Through collective action the impotent protest or insignificant exit of a single individual gives way to more powerful protest. But, as Pierre Bourdieu observes, the member of the protesting group runs the same risk she ran as a member of the institution being protested. Even as she achieves powerful speech by joining in a collective reforming effort, she risks being dispossessed of her own voice, joining in a common protesting voice that may not precisely match her specific point of view.[19]

In the wake of Clarence Thomas's Supreme Court confirmation hearings, many women in the United States were moved to think about reform activities. They were no longer content to accept a political system that was so unrepresentative of women. Immediately after the hearings, one particular small group of women got together to talk about ways that women and their voices could become a more influential part of the political process. Over a period of months the group expanded, increasing its base to make its reform effort more powerful. With this expansion, however, came the evolution of an agenda for the group that did not match that of some of the original members, and they dropped out. Reform groups, no less than other institutions, often offer the tradeoff between effectiveness and personal choice.

Reform is a term that carries a positive connotation. But reform can become subversion. There is a difference between reforming an institution's agenda and subverting the institution. One person's crusade to bring corporate expectations into line with her own agenda may often be seen by the institutional powers-that-be as subversion, as an attempt to wreck the institution. In practice, it may often be the case that reform (or subversion) is in the eye of the beholder. It is also possible that efforts to change an institution for the better can lead to results that all parties involved would agree are destructive. And, in the cases in which the alternatives of reform and subversion are most clearly posed, activists can embark on crusades that are intentionally subversive in character from the beginning.

One distinguishing characteristic between reforming and subverting an institution is the reformer's diagnosis of the problem. Are the efforts to change the institutional agenda based on a conviction that certain practices are at odds with the fundamental character of the institution? Or on a conviction that the essence of the institution itself is contrary to the reformer's personal morality? Related to the diagnosis of the problem is the intent of the reform efforts. Is the aim to improve the institution or to render it ineffective, perhaps abolish it completely? Reformist agendas are typically pursued openly. The criticisms are constructive, made in a spirit that recognizes the need for ongoing interpersonal relations to support the future functioning of the institution. The more subversive an actor's intent, the more likely it is that the activity will be hidden. The impulses become more destructive, aiming not to improve the institution but to undo it.

The distinction between reform and subversion is illustrated by civil disobedience, a device for political reform that can be distinguished from mere criminal behavior and revolutionary activity. Civil disobedience is illegal activity, but it is committed publicly, openly, to bring change to the political system. The resister is not subverting the legal system by acting secretly and attempting to evade detection. Rather he invites and accepts punishment in a process that strives to bring the law into conformity with justice. Civil disobedience is a nonviolent way of bringing change to the lawful regime rather than a violent, revolutionary attempt to overthrow it. As Martin Luther King, Jr., wrote from his cell in Birmingham:

> In no sense do I advocate evading or defying the law as the rabid segregationist would do. This would lead to anarchy. One who breaks an unjust law must do it *openly, lovingly* . . . and with a willingness to accept the penalty. I submit that an individual who breaks a law that conscience tells him is unjust, and willingly stays in jail to arouse the conscience of the community over its injustice, is in reality expressing the very highest respect for law.[20]

An interesting mix of these two approaches occurs when a reformer seeks to subvert particular aspects of the group's life in order to achieve an improvement in the whole. In such cases, the end is reformist—to enhance the institution—while the means are subversive—undermining or destroying specific aspects of the corporate agenda. Thus, for example, a citizen could act to try to render ineffective the implementation of a military draft or prevent the construction of a nuclear power plant or defy the collection of income tax, thinking the country would be better off if these things weren't done.

A combination of factors leads potential reformers down the more subversive paths: less loyalty to established group process, less faith in the willingness of the institution to respond positively to reform proposals, a greater willingness to take the exit option if the subversive scheme is exposed or ineffective. In general, these add up to less commitment to and less confidence in the institutional agenda and those who control it.

Institutional problems that are especially entrenched and pervasive may require action that is nothing short of rebellion. William Scott and David Hart call for that kind of response to the dominance in our society of the "organizational imperative," the notion that persons are to act for the good of institutions:

> The organizational imperative is the basis of both educational curricula and administration, from grade school to graduate school. It is the centerpiece of the moral orthodoxy of contemporary management, which means that it provides the justification for virtually all management decisions in all sectors. It provides the lingua franca of the articles and books used to train managers and to improve orga-

nizational performance. Finally, the reputations of most management scholars and practitioners are based upon their expertise in the applications of the organizational imperative. They are the defenders of the faith. Though disputed it may be, the organizational imperative is still deeply entrenched in American life, and our leaders persist in planning our future in its terms. Unless we rebel, we will continue to follow a lie.[21]

They call for a revolution that must begin by refusing to live in servitude to institutional agendas, insisting that institutions are justified only as they promote the health and actualization of individuals.

If John, the member of the exclusive country club, wants to reform that club's institutional expectations regarding exclusionary membership practices, he has several options available to him. The first reform option is working within channels. There may be a number of acceptable routes within the club for expressing his concern. He could ask the club's leadership about the existing membership policies and practices, indicating his own uneasiness about the resulting composition of the membership. Informal conversation with other club members may uncover allies and give courage to others to speak their minds. The club may have a formal process through which resolutions or new polices could be proposed. In his own member nomination activities, or through inclusion on the membership committee, John may be able to raise awareness of and increase sensitivity to his personal agenda.

A second option available to John is to blow the whistle on the club. While the fact that the club's membership is all white may be well known in the community at large, the game changes when someone makes an issue of it. The news media may become an important tool. As an insider, John can point out how little value should be given to the lack of a formal discrimination statement in the official policies, emphasizing the real expectations he and other club members feel. Disclosures can put pressure on elected officials, presidents of educational institutions, ministers, prominent civic leaders, and others who may find public association with discriminatory practices to be an embarrassment. Similarly, organizations with institutional memberships or which hold functions at the club may be dissuaded from continuing association. Club members who had easily compartmentalized their lives may find it more difficult to maintain that separation when faced with media scrutiny and public criticism.

The third option of exit with voice may not significantly enhance the effectiveness of John's reform efforts. Unless he is a exceptionally powerful and influential member (in which case one of the first two options would likely have been successful), the club will not be damaged by the loss of one member. The resignation could be worth one extra headline in the morning paper. His separation from the club may add some credibility to his protest in the eyes of some observers, and it could resolve some lingering doubts in his own mind about his membership. Other members might follow his lead in resigning. But exit with voice must be chosen carefully, as it is an option that can (usually) only be exercised once. In general, the effect of a club member resigning in protest will be less than the effect of the resignation of someone such as a cabinet member or the physicist directing a national nuclear energy program.

Subversion would be John's last alternative. The subversive efforts could focus on the membership practices. The tactics available to him would depend on the way the club's membership process functions. It may be possible to undermine the process by delaying tactics: challenging presented information, questioning references, mounting extended debate. Meetings could be disrupted or complicated on procedural grounds. If the club requires a supermajority for admission decisions, a minority could be marshalled to block all new members. Legal action could be brought which, even if ultimately unsuccessful, would be costly to the club in several different ways: expense, publicity, diversion of time and energy.

A broader subversive strategy would expand its target beyond the membership process to the club itself. The civilized decorum that is a prime amenity of private clubs could be shattered. John could disrupt life at the club through uncooperative acts in scheduling and reservations or demands for services. He could harass the leadership through nitpicking insistence on compliance with existing rules or bylaws. Broader legal challenges would be possible to question, for example, the property tax treatment of the club including its appraised value or the discriminatory treatment of employees. The club is dependent upon a flow of goods, services, and personnel from the outside which may give the subversive another source of leverage.

The subversive John may, of course, be expelled. Even this result could fit into his reforming scheme if he had concluded that expulsion would attract more attention and, perhaps, more sympathy than would resigning in protest. John's decisions about which type of reform tactics to pursue will depend on his assessment of the situation and his commitment to change. And, if reform is not forthcoming, then he will be faced with a new set of decisions.

A major problem in being a reformer is that it is hard work. Few people can devote the passion and energy needed to sustain crusading activities over a long period of time or a wide range of institutions. A reformer usually is required to make sacrifices, sometimes great sacrifices, in family life, vocational advancement, financial security, or other aspects of personal life. Reform efforts do not always succeed, despite considerable investment and commitment. Reformers sometimes discover that their efforts were misguided or that the benefit was not worth the cost.

A second problem that can accompany reform activities is what Eric Mount has termed "obsessions": "They can easily lower us. We seek people and groups to blame and preclude the possibility that they may have some redeeming qualities. We succumb to a creeping blindness to the ambivalence of our motives and the mixed results of our actions."[22] Because reform can be so difficult to achieve and because the personal costs can be so great, this task can often be taken up only by those who are obsessed with a cause. Those who see both sides of every issue rarely take to the streets. Those who always see value in the status quo and risk in unknown futures are not inclined to put themselves on the line for change. Holy crusades are always to be feared, but many needed crusades will never come to pass without reformers who believe that their cause is holy.

Reinhold Niebuhr stated this paradox most eloquently in the closing passage of *Moral Man and Immoral Society:* "[J]ustice cannot be approximated if the hope of its perfect realization does not generate a sublime madness in the soul. Nothing but such madness will do battle with malignant power and 'spiritual wickedness in high places.' The illusion is dangerous because it encourages terrible fanaticism. It must therefore be brought under the control of reason. One can only hope that reason will not destroy it before its work is done."[23] Not all reformers engage in the task of redeeming society, which is the target of Niebuhr's remarks. Many reforming responses to institutional agendas may, in fact, seem trivial by comparison. But all efforts for reform share in common a conviction that one's own truth should take precedence over that of others.

For these reasons the reformer's response to the conflict between institutional and personal agendas is not one to be entered into lightly. However, when the conflict is significant, when commitment to one's personal agenda is unshakable and loyalty to the institution is firm (or when the institution is seen as essential to advancing one's personal agenda), the response of the reformer may be the only option that can be chosen with integrity.

8

The Accommodator

Sullivan Ballou, a soldier in the Union army during the American Civil War, wrote a letter to his wife in 1861. The eloquence and passion of this portrait of the two loves of his life captured the heart of a nation—or at least the forty million of us who had tuned in—as his letter was read as part of PBS's showing of Ken Burns's documentary, "The Civil War." The only way to convey the spirit of this letter is to reproduce it in its entirety:

Headquarters
Camp Clark
Washington, D.C.
July 14, 1861

My Very Dear Wife
The indications are very strong that we shall move in a few days perhaps tomorrow and lest I should not be able to write you again I feel impelled to write a few lines that may fall under your eye when I am no more. Our movement may be one of a few days duration and be full of pleasure. And it may be one of severe conflict and death to me. "Not my will be thine O God be done." If it is necessary that I should fall on the battle field for my Country I am ready. I have no misgivings about or lack of confidence in the cause which I am engaged, and my courage does not halt or falter. I know how American Civilization now bears upon the triumph of the Government and how great a debt we owe to those who went before us through the blood and suffering of the Revolution; and I am willing perfectly willing to lay down all my joys in this life to help maintain this Government and to pay that debt.

But my dear wife, when I know that with my own joys I lay down nearly all of yours, and replace them in this life with care and sorrow when after having eaten for long years the bitter fruit of orphanage myself, I must offer it as their only sustenance to my dear little children. Is it weak or dishonorable that while the banner of purpose flotes calmly and proudly in the breeze, underneath my unbounded love for you my dear wife and children should struggle in fierce though useless contest with my love of Country.

I cannot describe to you my feelings on this calm summer night when two thousand men are sleeping around me, many of them enjoying the last perhaps before that of Death. And I suspicion that Death is creeping behind me with his fatal dart am communing with God my Country and thee. I have sought most closely and diligently and often in my brest for a wrong motive in this hazarding the happiness of all that I love and I could not find one. A pure love of my Country and of the principels I have advocated before the people and the name of honor that I love more than I fear death have called upon me and I have obeyed.

Sarah my love for you is deathless it seems to bind me with mighty cables that nothing but Omnipotence can break. And yet my love of Country comes over me like a strong wind and bears me irresistibly with all those chains to the battlefield. The memories of the blissful moments I have enjoyed with you come crouding over me, and I feel most deeply grateful to God and you that I have enjoyed them so long. And how hard it is for me to give them up and burn to ashes the hopes of future years when God willing we might still have loved and loved together and see our boys grow up to honourable manhood around us. I know I have but few claims upon Divine Providence but something whispers to me perhaps it is the wafted prayer of my little Edgar that I shall return to my loved ones unharmed. If I do not my dear Sarah never forget how much I loved you nor that when my last breath escapes me on the battlefield it will whisper your name.

Forgive my many faults and the many pains I have caused you. How thoughtless how foolish I have sometimes been! How gladly would I wash out with my tears every little spot upon your happiness and strugle with all the misfortunes of this world to shield you and my children from harm but I cannot. I must watch you from the spirit world and hover near you while you buffet the storms with your precious little freight—and wait with sad patience till we meet to part no more.

But Oh Sarah! If the dead can come back to this earth and flit unseen around those they love I shall be always with you in the brightest day and the darkest night amidst your happiest scenes, and gloomiest hours *always always* and when the soft breeze fans your cheek it shall be my breath or the cool air your throbbing temple it shall be my spirit passing by. Sarah do not mourn me dead. Think I am gone and wait for me for we shall meet again.

As for my little boys they will grow up as I have done and never know a fathers love and care. Little Willie is to young to remember me long but my blue eyed Edgar will keep my frolics with him among the dimmest memories of his childhood. Sarah I have unlimited confidence in your maternal care and your development of their characters. Tell my two mothers I call Gods blessings upon them. Oh! Sarah I wait for you *then* come to me and lead thither my children.

Sullivan[1]

Ballou's response to the conflicting agendas of family and country embodied in this letter is unlike any we have encountered in previous chapters. He does not simply choose one agenda or the other. While he has physically left his wife to follow the army's call, no fair reading of this letter could conclude that he had compartmentalized his life, creating a distinct sphere in which the claims of one agenda do not intrude into the realm of another. He went south with the army, without attempting to reform its expectations of him.

This letter typifies a response that is inclusive, that tries to embrace conflicting claims rather than pick one and exclude others. The effort is to view these claims as competing rather than irreconcilably contradictory. His impulse was to expand his possibilities, to be open and receptive to clashing values, to accommodate as best he could the expectations that he felt were valid, however incompatible they were with one another. Such an approach is not an easy one, especially when one of the institutions is as far-reaching in its claims as the United States Army. In this particular instance, some may view with skepticism the success of Major Ballou's accommodator strategy—he was killed shortly after writing the letter. It seems that an assessment of his choice could only be made, however, after seeing the letter his wife might have written in response to his.

The accommodator views the other types of responses to conflicting agendas as, for the most part, impossibly simplistic. The either/or choices of the "hermit," the "institutionalized person," and the "split personality" are seen as divisions that are too neat, given the complexity of our lives. The "reformer's" position, as a pure type, reflects a naiveté about the realities of social institutions. The accommodator's choice of a viable, enduring response is one that grapples with the persuasiveness and intransigence of institutional agendas.

The accommodator differs from the hermit in that she accepts participation in institutions as a given. Her involvement in a corporate setting may result from a need to fulfill personal agendas, for example, the obligation to provide material goods for one's family. Or involvement may come from a decision to use institutions as best one can to accomplish important social, political, or economic goals. Corporate involvement may be little more than a realization that we all participate in institutions to some degree or another, and the question is only one of how much to participate rather than whether to participate. In this way, the accommodator sees herself as more realistic than the hermit, accepting institutional involvement as an inevitable reality of modern life.

The accommodator differs from the institutionalized person in that he maintains some autonomy of value, some commitment to personal choice and control; the accommodator will not put his own judgment on the shelf. The difference between surrender and accommodation is the difference that separates these two types. While an accommodator strategy recognizes that external demands will play a role in shaping the final decision, he insists that one's personal agenda will also play a part in that decision.

The split personality approach could be seen as a kind of accommodation. An example provided by Carol Gilligan will illustrate the difference between the type of compromise embraced by the split personality and the approaches described in this chapter. Two four-year-olds—a girl and a boy—wanted to play different games. The girl suggested playing next-door neighbors, but the boy responded that he wanted to play pirates. "Okay," replied the girl, "then you can be the pirate that lives next door." A fair solution of taking turns and playing each game for an equal period would have been a kind of split personality response. The solution suggested

by the girl, an option termed an inclusive solution by Gilligan, is in
the accommodator spirit. As she observes:

> The fair solution, taking turns, leaves the identity of each game
> intact. It provides an opportunity for each child to experience the oth-
> er's imaginative world and regulates the exchanges by imposing a
> rule based on the premise of equal respect. The inclusive solution, in
> contrast, transforms both games: the neighbor game is changed by
> the presence of a pirate living next door; the pirate game is changed
> by bringing the pirate into the neighborhood. Each child not only en-
> ters the other's imaginative world but also transforms that world by
> his or her presence. The identity of each separate game yields to a
> new combination, since the relationship between the children gives
> rise to a game that neither had separately imagined.[2]

The accommodator differs from the split personality in
that she is not willing to surrender even some part of her life to
institutional control. The clash of two agendas will yield a new
agenda, not a division of time or space between two old ones. She
is convinced that personal morality has something to say about all
aspects of one's life, and she sees a moral dimension to all that she
does. She is driven by a need to keep her eye fixed on that guiding
star of personal morality, knowing that her choice will be affected
by accommodating the views of others.

The accommodator, however, may be more tired than the
reformer, or maybe he is more cynical, more realistic, weaker. For
whatever reason, this person accepts the conclusion that institutional expectations will never be changed to coincide with his
personal agenda. Thus, the accommodator finds himself staying in
an institutional environment, by tacit consent if nothing else, participating in and supporting a corporate agenda that contains elements that are incongruent with his personal values. But he
chooses this option knowing that at this time and in this place, this
choice seems to "optimize" his personal agenda. So he chooses to
balance various personal norms, needs, and interests against the
costs of continued membership. The accommodator doesn't forget
the differences; he doesn't sit *too* easily in the institution. He is not
adverse to taking opportunities to make changes when they appear,
but he knows that even those moments present opportunities that
are small, partial, and temporary. And in the meantime, he is just
doing what he can.

Accommodation is a term that is not held in high esteem by many people in today's world. It often evokes an image of weaklings compromising important principles, of selling out and giving in. Thoughts about accommodators evoke the memories of concession after concession being made to Adolph Hitler as he expanded the boundaries of the Third Reich. In this light, accommodators appear to be concerned with prudence rather than morality, with escaping responsibility rather than living up to it. Such concerns are important, pointing out that this approach can be misused—as is the case with any of the alternatives.

Compromise is an activity full of promise and threat.[3] Compromise holds the promise of doing as much that is morally good as could be expected, leaving open the possibility of even more good in the future. This is achieved while acting within a mutual respect for the dignity and freedom of all persons, a respect that creates and sustains a community in which we can live cooperatively together. On the other hand, compromise holds the danger of tragedy and tyranny, of capitulation, self-deception or co-optation in which core moral values are abandoned and power is surrendered to those who are untrustworthy. While the accommodator's style of dealing with conflicting agendas does not guarantee a response that others will find morally acceptable, this choice can be framed in a positive way that embodies elements that are recognized as worthwhile.

Three of the definitions of the word *accommodate* give meaning to three different types of action that fall under this category. The first meaning has to do with harmonizing and reconciling, making adjustments for others with different points of view, *accommodating differences*. The second meaning is one of adaptation, making suitable in light of surroundings, *accommodating oneself* to circumstances. Third is the notion of making room for, supplying space, *providing accommodations*. These three senses of the term provide a basis for thinking about the responses of three categories of accommodators: (1) the "arbitrator"; (2) the "improvisor" and the "calculator"; and (3) the "pluralist," respectively. As we look at the nuances in differences among the approaches, remember that we will rarely encounter one of these ideal types of responses in its pure form, without signs of other types.

The Arbitrator

The arbitrator or negotiator, when faced with institutional expectations that would constrain personal choice, chooses neither to escape the institutional limitations nor to surrender to them, but to work within the system, eliminating contradictions and reconciling differences as best he can. Accommodation in this sense is making adjustments for others with different agendas. In each situation, this negotiator is discovering, evaluating, and weighing items from the agendas of others. The method is avowedly one of compromise, seeking the best that can be achieved within the confines of the specific situation. "Best" is probably determined by reference to the core values of the arbitrator's personal agenda but only after those expectations have been modified by what is judged to be feasible or realistic within a particular institution at a particular time. The combined tactics of modifying personal agendas in light of institutional realities and seeking institutional action that is optimal in terms of personal values results in a give-and-take that the negotiator hopes will produce an acceptable truce in the conflict. Theological ethicists have sometimes referred to this as a "middle axiom approach,"[4] accepting, for example, the standard of justice when the radical demands of love cannot be fulfilled in a social or political setting.

Allan Gibbard has referred to the norms that emerge from this kind of process as the "norms of the second best."[5] He characterizes these agendas of accommodation as the best anyone could hope for—norms for circumstances of a special kind, when groups are living in deep disagreement, and workable compromises when no acceptable alternative exists. It is understood that they are not the best possible norms, but when there is no consensus about what is best, this reconciling approach does offer an agenda that is stabilizing and more or less attainable. Life's chief quandary for Gibbard is when to accept norms of accommodation and when to reject them, knowing that they can be a "covenant with death and an agreement with hell," as William Lloyd Garrison characterized the United States' accommodation of slavery.[6]

David Fritzsche has provided a model that can serve as an example of one form of arbitrating between personal values and institutional imperatives. In this model, minimum cutoff points are established for acceptable behavior based on one's ethical concerns and based on institutional (that is, economic, technological, political) concerns. Once a particular set of alternatives being considered clears the ethical minimum, then choices among those alternatives are guided by the nonmoral factors. Ethics sets the floor (although it's not clear what happens when all institutionally viable alternatives are below this floor), then other considerations take over, meaning that "some business decisions are made which when considered on the ethics dimension alone would be immediately rejected."[7]

Sometimes this process of accommodation looks like an "ethics of the gaps." Institutional agendas are not all-encompassing; they do not rigidly specify in great detail every decision, every action to be taken by the group's members. Corporate agendas leave some pertinent matters unaddressed or leave room for personal discretion. Social expectations must be interpreted, leaving open the possibility of imaginative and creative personal appropriation of those group expectations. Thus, we believe that individuals do make a difference in organizations. Responding to the same corporate agendas from the same position, two different people will engage in interpretation, exercises of discretion, and compromises that yield different results.

One of the reasons individuals often choose to remain in institutional settings that are not wholly compatible with their personal agendas is the perception that "hanging in there" can expand their power to implement their personal agenda within the institution. This expansion comes in a formal way as one moves up the organizational ladder. Higher ranking positions typically offer greater opportunities to put one's own principles into action. In a complex organization as one moves from a staff position to a line position to a policy-making position, one's ability to exert influence on the institutional agenda is enhanced. In a different kind of institution, the family, teenagers become clan matriarchs and patriarchs (although in this context the length of service sometimes reverses the flow of power as adult children eventually find themselves parenting their parents). The assumption of more responsible positions over time—in families, military units, or corporations—increases the weight of personal agendas in the bargaining process.

One's institutional history can also provide a basis for

changing the negotiating balance in informal ways as well. People learn how to manage the system rather than be managed by it. Personal IOUs accumulate. Experience teaches: how and when risks can be taken; which institutional expectations are unyielding and which only appear to be so; which organizational orders are serious and which are pro forma exercises; where the institutional tolerance for exceptions lies.

Equipped with knowledge of this kind, the arbitrator negotiates her way through the institution's agenda, accepting as reality the limits that are fixed with the understanding and satisfaction that her personal values are having an effect on the reconciliation and adjustment that is taking place. As long as the impenetrable barriers are not too great and the compromises are good enough, the arbitrator has avoided the contradictions that would create the need to choose a different response.

What would it mean for John, who faces the dilemma described earlier, to respond as an arbitrator? John would seek to find some compromise between his personal beliefs in equality and the policies and practices of his club. He would work within the club's existing structure, trying to reduce the differences as best he could. Possibilities might exist for honorary or associate memberships or other kinds of special affiliations that would not be so rigidly exclusionary. He could find openings to pursue implementation of employment policies within the club that reflected a greater sensitivity to concerns about discrimination. He could seek certain positions within the club's hierarchy that would allow him to stop the perpetuation of social practices that are perceived to be rooted in prejudicial attitudes. The club could even associate itself with community programs that addressed the problems that divide our society without, of course, directly challenging the exclusionary membership practices.

An arbitrator often attempts to balance competing demands, searching for an acceptable middle path. John may accept an exception: commitment to equal treatment except when it conflicts with legitimate concerns about privacy and freedom of association. Or somewhere between his personal commitment to equal treatment and the club's expectation of a homogenous membership may lie some compromise norm of not actively foreclosing the possibility of nonwhite members. John could hope for the day when the institutional culture would permit a real integration of its membership. This hope, however, would not result in a reformer's crusade but in an incrementalism which relied on an expectation that someday the time will be right. He would position himself so that he could help influence the course of events when that time came. If John can see some possibilities for narrowing the gap between the two agendas, he may well be content with this approach, feeling that he has done the best he could under the circumstances.

The Improvisor

The improvisor travels lightly. Living more out of imagination than regulation, the improvisor responds to conflicts between personal and institutional agendas with a willingness to reassess continually the articles of his personal morality. In each moment new understandings and consequent reformulations of the personal agenda are possible—even anticipated. Recalling the second definition of *accommodate,* the theme is adaptation, making appropriate responses in light of one's circumstances.

Mary Catherine Bateson has caught the essence of this notion, describing improvisation as "discovering the shape of our creation along the way, rather than pursuing a vision already defined." Writing about the lives of five women as works-in-progress, she features a view of life as adaptation to a landscape that is in constant flux, as refiguring familiar material in new ways, ways that are especially sensitive to context, interaction, and response.[8] This fluid, evolving response to circumstances may be risky, but it is rich with the potential of new possibilities.

Institutional expectations form personal agendas. Personal norms are given their meaning only in concrete situations. "Circumstances alter rules and principles," as Joseph Fletcher describes situation ethics.[9] When we move from one institution to another, or as the agenda of a group to which we belong changes, our situation changes in ways that raise the prospect of a revised meaning for our personal agenda. We cannot know in advance the dynamics of a unique moment—and all moments are unique to some degree. Thus, in this view, we cannot predict with certainty what our personal agenda will require. So, we improvise. We read the situation, mine the context for clues, and the strongest clues will be the expectations embodied in our institutional settings.

The improvisor's response, however, is not the same as that of the institutionalized person. Adapting one's personal agenda to a specific setting is not the same as simply accepting the expectations of a particular institution. Improvising is not abdicating responsibility for choice but is accepting responsibility for choosing in a fashion appropriate to one's surroundings. The personal agenda is informed by context, not replaced by an authority in the context.

It is this combination of maintaining a personal agenda yet changing it to fit new situations that makes the improvisor vulnerable to the phenomenon Michael Walzer has called the "problem of dirty hands." Walzer's discussion focuses on political life, but the dilemma he identifies arises in other arenas of life. This problem is not a special feature of some mysterious "political sphere" but is inherent in the practice of morality.[10] The example Walzer uses to illustrate this problem, which we looked at in chapter 7, is that of an election candidate who must make a deal with a dishonest ward boss involving the granting of contracts for school construction over the next four years, in order to win the election. He is extremely reluctant even to consider the deal because he has the kind of scruples that lead us to know that he is a good man.[11]

Walzer's assessment is that, given the importance of the campaign, we hope he will overcome his scruples and make the deal: "It is important to stress that we don't want just *anyone* to make the deal; we want *him* to make it precisely because he has scruples about it. *We know he is doing right when he makes the deal because he knows he is doing wrong.*" What distinguishes this response from that of the split personality and even that of the arbitrator is that this politician will believe himself to be guilty. He has not acted in an area in which his personal agenda does not apply, nor has he negotiated a satisfactory compromise between his personal norms and institutional expectations. He is a guilty man. He has committed a moral offense, and his willingness to acknowledge and bear his guilt is evidence "that he is not too good for politics and that he is good enough."[12]

Why is the improvisor a candidate for feeling such guilt when the arbitrator does not? Why can the arbitrator seek to avoid contradictions through reconciliation and adjustment, while the improvisor may well be called to accept and anguish over moral contradictions? The improvisor acts out of a personal agenda that has been modified by an encounter with new circumstances. The good person who becomes a politician would not have made deals with dishonest ward bosses until he found himself in a situation in which such a deal seemed right. This accommodation involves adapting one's moral choices to be appropriate in new circumstances.

If the personal agenda, as it existed prior to entering the new situation, were to be regarded as something like a guideline for negotiating decisions, then the compromise can be viewed more positively. The arbitrator may feel a certain pride in negotiating the best compromise available. The improvisor, on the other hand, may experience this reality in a different way, as described by Walzer: "When rules are overridden, we do not talk or act as if they had been set aside, canceled, or annulled. They still stand and have this much effect at least: that we know we have done something wrong even if what we have done was also the best thing to do on the whole in the circumstances."[13] The personal agenda stays with the improvisor. She may act in a given situation as if new facts had transformed the meaning of that agenda, and after the fact she may be convinced that the best choice was made. But this choice is not made without a cost incurred by the loss of a moral conviction that was her own. This is a painful process, weighing the wrong that one is willing to do in order to do right.

Is it necessary for the improvisor to suffer this anguish? If one's agenda is continually reinterpreted in light of changing circumstances and the changing institutional agendas they bring, is this feeling of guilt an inherent part of the improvisor's response? Walzer describes agonizing that is painful, but it is this suffering, this uncertainty and self-questioning that distinguish the improvisor from the institutionalized person. Without this continued memory of and fidelity to the personal agenda that precedes the situation at hand, the personal agenda becomes captive to institutional expectations. In such cases, the individual loses the anchor that keeps personal choice from being a mere reflection of group pressures.

The ever-present temptation in the improvisor's approach to conflicting agendas is to follow the corporate wisdom present in each new situation. The pull of this inclination becomes stronger as the pain of acknowledging and accepting guilt increases. It is this pain, however, that reminds the responder that this is an accommodation to specific new situations, not a surrender to them. As such, a role must continue to exist for the personal agenda to bring values to each moment that have their source outside of the particular set of circumstances.

I have a lot of friends who have thought of themselves as children of the sixties. These people did a lot of their growing up between 1963 and 1970. During that time they assaulted the "establishment." They didn't trust anyone over thirty and preached a message of peace and love. While some now appear simply to have rejected the creed of their youth, others strike me as improvisors. As their world has changed, they have reformulated or reinterpreted their beliefs and values. The expectations of the institutions that now define their lives—parenthood, the church, the office and factory, the political party—have led to behaviors that seemed unimaginable not so long ago. But the memory remains. There is a sense of betrayal, of having allowed a contamination of the purity of the earlier vision.

As with Walzer's politician, the feeling of guilt is not enough to force a different decision. The rationalizations are too good for that. The explanations about the appropriateness of the new versions of personal values in the new world of responsibilities are too convincing. The sense of loss, however, continues to serve as a reminder that they should not be too comfortable in this world of grown-ups. And, on occasion, this improvisor may act in a way that is inexplicable, save for the thought that in 1968 he could not have imagined acting otherwise.

For John the improvisor, the conflict between his country club's practices and his personal expectations provides an occasion for him to reassess the meaning of equal treatment of persons. His efforts to adapt to these circumstances would lead to a revised personal agenda, based on a conclusion that his earlier understanding of equal treatment was unsophisticated, too naive or simplistic, or overly rigid. He would use his vantage point within the club to view the issue within the wider scope of a broader network of human relationships and needs.

John's search for a "new" meaning for equal treatment could consider such possibilities as: equal treatment as requiring affirmative efforts to compensate for the continuing effects of unequal treatment by others in the past; equal treatment as a duty to see that institutional practices do not result in unfavorable results for people because of their race; equal treatment as institutional procedural correctness that does not overtly exclude or disadvantage anyone on the grounds of race; equal treatment as a personal commitment to avoid harming others because of their race; equal treatment as a concern, among others, that should be considered in structuring human relationships. John will not surrender his choice of the meaning of equal treatment to the club's authorities, but his own choice will be influenced to the degree he is committed to his club membership.

As John modifies his expectation of what equal treatment requires, he will be aware of what he is doing. The result will not be an accommodation that leaves him feeling good, but one that he knows is less than it could have been. He has not abandoned the personal agenda item of treating people fairly, but the significance of that commitment may well have been diminished. John may believe that this is the most acceptable choice, given the competing claims on him, but it remains a choice he would have preferred that he did not have to make.

The Calculator

Another option exists for accommodation in light of particular social contexts. This option involves not a changing of one's personal agenda, in the way of the improvisor, but the development of a personal agenda that relies on a commitment to certain *formal* moral standards, leaving to each situation the task of filling in the *content.* A person taking such an approach could be considered a calculator, in the sense of employing a scheme somewhat like the utilitarian calculus described by Jeremy Bentham.[14]

The calculator could, for example, expect that he would act in a way that would promote the greatest good for the greatest number of people. One of his things to do could be understood as generally doing whatever results in the largest balance of good over evil in any particular situation. Obviously the precise nature of his actions is dependent upon the features of a concrete set of circumstances. Each time he is called upon to choose and act, he calculates which response will produce the best results.

This approach, a classical utilitarian approach, has in common with the improvisor's model the feature that circumstances shape the meaning of personal agendas. Like the improvisor, the calculator brings personal expectations to the situation, but the content and significance of those expectations take shape only in particular social contexts, and the reality of institutional restraints is accepted. Thus, when a conflict between a personal and an institutional agenda can be tolerated by calculating the best one can do in a particular setting this responder will be satisfied with that.

Sometimes a person can be heard to say something like: I should have done X, but I did Y. Initially this seems puzzling, particularly in those cases in which the individual seems quite content, even pleased, with the choice of doing Y. It seems to me that the part of the statement, "I should have done X," really means something like: I think X would have been the best response in an ideal world, and I wish the facts of the case had been such that I could have chosen that, but they were not.

We do not, of course, live in an ideal world. We cannot design the circumstances in which we act or determine the facts of the situations in which we choose. The person who is satisfied with having done Y recognizes these realities, accepting that acting out of a personal agenda means shaping her expectations of herself in light of such social contexts as institutional expectations.

While the calculator shares the improvisor's willingness to adapt to institutional agendas, this responder does not share the improvisor's guilt. The improvisor recalls a personal agenda that was modified by new circumstances and feels some remorse about what was lost in that modification. The calculator's personal agenda contains less that can be lost. It anticipates and is given shape only as the new circumstances are faced. This difference can be seen by looking at Walzer's election candidate who must make a deal with a dishonest ward boss to win an election. The calculator focuses on the consequences of making different decisions. What result can be predicted from a choice to make a deal? What result can be predicted from a choice not to make a deal? The two outcomes are compared, the politician determines which outcome is preferable, and the decision is made. The right decision has been made. The best result available to the decision-maker has been achieved. When presented with Walzer's "dirty hands" problem, the calculator's response is, "What problem?" Rather than feeling guilty about having committed a moral offense (if the choice is to make the deal), the calculator is pleased that he has done the right thing.[15]

We saw this same satisfaction with doing the best that can be achieved in the response of the arbitrator. In each case, the decision-maker is modifying her expectations in an encounter with a particular institution at a particular time. The distinction between these two responses lies in the nature of the personal agenda. The arbitrator's agenda includes expectations rooted in certain non-consequential considerations, such as: I expect to keep promises I make; I expect to be honest in my dealings with customers; I expect to avoid torturing my children. The arbitrator comes to the institutional setting with these rather definite expectations, and alters them as they conflict with other group expectations to the contrary. The alteration is one of compromise. The original agenda still exerts an influence, a pull to come up with a reconciliation as close to this list of things to do as possible.

The calculator, in a pure sense,[16] does not bring such a defined list to the moment of decision. Keeping promises, dealing honestly with others, and avoiding the torture of children have a moral pull for him only if, in a given context, acting in these ways can be shown to produce the best results of all available courses of action. He may enter the situation with expectations, based on past experience, that keeping promises, dealing honestly, and avoiding torture will usually lead to desirable consequences. These summaries of experience or rules of thumb, however, are not obligatory expectations and can be readily overridden by a calculation that lying, cheating, or torturing will produce better results. The arbitrator, therefore, is engaged in a negotiation between his agenda and that of the institution, while the calculator is projecting the effect institutional expectations (and the means of enforcing those expectations) will have on the consequences of certain acts.

Let us return to John as he assesses the conflict between personal and institutional norms. For John the calculator, the commitment to equal treatment of persons means that he would identify this as one goal to be aimed for, among others. In trying to determine the balance of good over bad, John would identify the enhancement of equal treatment as being a good aspect of a possible outcome. John has also identified other desirable results that he would factor into his calculation, results that are associated with the club's agenda: that personal privacy be respected; that individual choice be as unrestrained as possible; that fellowship with family and close friends be fostered; that people benefit from the recreational facilities and services of the club.

If John pursues an accommodator strategy in the end, he will do so because he reached a conclusion that the benefits of this compromise outweigh the benefits (including the calculation of costs) of other options. He could conclude that the real impact on the cause of equal treatment of him, one individual, staying in the exclusive club is negligible. The benefits to him and his family are considerable. While the situation is not ideal when judged by his personal agenda, putting up with this club's membership policy is justified by the results.

The calculating approach may not always result in accommodation. As John tests each available response by looking at likely consequences, other conclusions are possible. He may conclude that the greater good will be achieved by working for reform through channels, going public with his complaint, or quitting in protest. In such cases, calculation is a means to choosing a type of response other than an accommodator strategy. Nevertheless, this presentation of the calculating response does seems to fit in a chapter on accommodation. It describes an approach to compromise not contained within the other accommodating responses. Further, the features of a less determinate personal agenda and a willingness to do the best one can within given institutional structures seem to make accommodation likely in many instances.

The Pluralist

The third meaning of *accommodate* is to make room for. The pluralist wants to make room for as many perspectives as possible, to accommodate a variety of agendas. The pluralist's view is not that conflicting expectations can be harmonized, as is the case with the arbitrator, but that the differences that do exist can be put into perspective and are thus not so troublesome. This style of coming to terms with one's institutional setting often focuses on *process* rather than *results*. The pluralist emphasizes fidelity to personal agendas and lets the results fall where they may. If a divergence between institutional structure and personal agenda leads to an undesirable result, the response is something in the vein of, "It's not my problem," or at least, "It's not my fault." This approach places the concept of agenda faithfulness on center stage as the basis for evaluating one's behavior.

The pluralist's sense is that there will always be tasks that are undone, products that are unproduced. Final judgments thus may well rest not on the results of acts but on one's fidelity to principle in the process. This style takes very seriously the objection to the teleological approach that we do not control all the results of our actions. We can be true to our own values, but cannot presume to be accountable for consequences that are beyond our control. Furthermore, in the grand scheme of things, very little that one of us does in a given day has lasting significance in terms of results. The focal point therefore becomes how one lives.

An example of a pluralist was the public defender in New Orleans who put up with his job for three years.[17] Rick Teissier put up with long hours, juggling three hundred or more cases at a time, doing most of his own investigation and research without the basic tools of the profession. While he was still committed to his personal agenda of providing meaningful counsel to his clients, he accepted institutional priorities that made realization of his expectations impossible. Teissier himself eventually turned into a reformer. He refused to go to trial and prodded a judge to rule that he was incapable of providing his client an effective defense—a ruling that included a finding that the city's entire indigent defense program was unconstitutional. Many other individuals, however, continue to struggle to pursue personal agendas in impossible institutional settings.

It may be that these pluralists are able to persevere in their institutions because they have developed a "psychic distance"—an unwillingness to take responsibility for the consequences of their actions.[18] This psychic distance is especially prevalent in larger institutions that rely heavily on mediation, the acting of persons on behalf of other persons. Because of this mediation we do not know the consequences of our acts or we feel powerless to change the consequences. The result is a sense of accountability only for one's individual effort.

How would our friend John, as a pluralist, deal with his personal commitment to equal treatment of all persons and his membership in an exclusive country club? He would bring his black and Jewish friends to the club as guests. He would be clear about his own preference for a nondiscriminatory admission practice in conversation with other club members and cast his votes in favor of diversifying membership when he is given the opportunity. He would not, however, engage in a crusade to reform the club's policies, nor would he consider quitting if change is not forthcoming. He would try to be true to his own beliefs in his personal actions, recognizing that other points of view may control the institutional agenda.

This response to conflicting institutional agendas has a flavor of the split personality to it. The split personality's arrangement of the world can be thought of as a horizontal one, with different arenas of one's life placed side by side and a vertical line being drawn separating these segments of life into two groups. Some of them are subordinated to the institution's expectations and others governed by one's personal norms. The pluralist's division, by contrast, can be imagined as a one resulting from drawing a horizontal line. If the different arenas are placed side by side, the line that is drawn cuts through all of the segments, dividing each individual field of activity. Within each arena, each social setting, there are aspects for which one has personal responsibility and others for which one does not.

The pluralist aspires to conform her actions to her personal agenda even in the face of contrary institutional agendas. She does, however, accept the wheel in which she may be an insignificant cog. She may feel that she is a victim of circumstances while accepting the circumstances. This alienation from the results of one's creative efforts can lead to a passivity that marks the split personality, a tendency to surrender to one's role. When that happens then it seems that only one decision is being made: to join the group or not.[19] The pluralist's slogan is, "Don't worry about things you can't control." She is called to a personal integrity to make her own choices that are faithful to her own agenda. If she is in a group context in which those choices don't lead to desirable results, that's simply a fact of life.

The pluralist accommodates these differences by devaluing them. We all look past differences we encounter that we decide are not worth fighting about. The pluralist expands the number of agenda conflicts that aren't worth fighting about by focusing on personal fidelity to principle and recognizing that it is legitimate for other persons to be faithful to their divergent principles. In its more extreme form, this response slides into a relativism that considers anyone's moral principles to be as good as anyone else's. Such a reduction of a personal agenda to a matter of aesthetic whim would run counter to the notion of responsibility described earlier. Even when the pluralist remains firmly committed to a personal agenda that he is willing to articulate and defend, the choice is for a privatized morality that has limited effect on social institutions.

This accommodating approach responds to conflicts by decreasing their importance. Pluralists are most often going to find this response appropriate in instances in which an implicit judgment has already been made that the matters at stake, or one's ability to influence them, are not significant. We make room for the agendas of other people when they do not threaten our core values or when they serve to advance certain important items on our own agenda. For example, if John's exclusive country club becomes a Ku Klux Klan chapter, the pluralist who believes in equality will likely take the hermit's option and resign. The pluralist's hope is that he can carve out personal space within an institution in which he can be true to his own beliefs while tolerating institutional results that do not present too great an affront to that personal agenda.

Concluding Thoughts on Accommodation

Accommodation, in its various senses, means to serve, aid, assist, help. We all act in these ways as members of various institutions. In evaluating our accommodating actions, we address two important issues: (1) the choice of persons, groups, or institutions as the recipients of our aid, and (2) how much we give away. We cannot belong to every group, nor can we be equally giving to all the institutions to which we are connected. Further, as accommodators there must be limits to our accommodation, even to those bodies to which we are most devoted—lest we slip into the mode of the institutionalized person.

The degree of conflict that we encounter will influence which memberships we accept and will shape the way we maintain them. If the personal and institutional expectations are diametrically opposed, that gives us an indication that we should not join that institution or should quickly leave it. The distance between the group and personal expectations, and the importance of the items in dispute, will influence greatly our choices of affiliation and our willingness to compromise. The extent to which a person is faithful to an institutional agenda is a function of how committed one is to sharing a future with others in that institution or group. Institutional loyalty is the valuing of that institutional future, as weighed against the futures that are in store for other groups. The greater our loyalty to an institution the greater will be the flexibility in our personal positions, meaning that we will more readily engage in accommodation.

Loyalty is a function not only of compatibility in values, but of the institution's effectiveness in serving desired purposes including, perhaps, the institutional benefits which accrue to us personally. Institutional flexibility is another important factor. Those bodies that are more open to our values, that offer greater prospects for change, will elicit greater individual efforts at reconciling differences. Evaluations of our personal effectiveness, of opportunities to exercise individual creativity in particular settings, affect how much we are willing to give and where we will give it.

Personal characteristics feed into an individual's aptitude for accommodation. How certain am I of my own conclusions? How much do I need the wisdom and experienced judgment of others? How willing am I to take the reformer's risk of being expelled or marginalized? How will an accommodating approach sit with my conscience? Deciding to pursue a strategy of accommodation does not yield automatic answers. In each encounter, the mixture of a unique moment, a specific individual, and a particular institution will yield a judgment that is not clearly indicated at the outset by the choice of an accommodating type of response. One is called to make assessments continually—juggling interests, drawing fine lines, walking tightropes. This flexibility sometimes makes this an attractive style of response, while this lack of certainty sometimes makes it an intolerable style of response.

9

The Convert

Sometimes a person encounters a conflict between personal and institutional agendas, stops to examine both agendas critically, and concludes, "I was wrong." In such cases the individual makes a conscious, considered decision to change her personal norms to match the institution's expectations. Unlike the "institutionalized person," who unreflectively accepts the institutional agenda, the "convert" looks at both sides of the value conflict before concluding that the group's point of view is preferable. This response also differs from the accommodator strategies. While the latter entail compromises and half-measures, the convert's response is a wholehearted acceptance of the institution's norms. The convert comes to the situation with a fully formed personal norm, encounters a contrary institutional norm, and decides that an appropriate response is the rejection of the prior personal norm.

The likelihood of conversion is especially high for young people who are often more actively involved in the continuing project of reevaluating their own agendas, and for those who are entering new institutions and exposing themselves to new expectations and possibilities. Thus, the freshman year in college is a particularly fertile time for conversion experiences. I went off to college in 1965. The last thing my hometown preacher said to me before I left was, "Don't go up there and get liberal on us." He recognized that in the 1960s many young people coming out of conservative upbringings were entering institutions of higher education, meeting a different set of expectations on a variety of issues (including racial tolerance, sexual activity, and military service), and converting.

I have been told the story of an executive in a religious

publishing house who entered the business full of idealism about a
particular mission for the firm. He crusaded for a publishing agenda
that would put the issues of peace and justice before the press's
readers, believing that this message must be promoted regardless of
what reader surveys and sales records showed about the preferences of potential readers. His approach encountered opposition
from those in power for whom the institution's first agenda item
was generating enough revenue to be self-supporting. Through the
years a conversion took place. The young staff member has become a chief executive, and he now argues with considerable conviction that the press should serve its readers by meeting their
needs and that the best measure of their needs is what they buy. It
may be an unfair overstatement to conclude that this man has
adopted, contrary to the spirit of the movie *Field of Dreams,* the
maxim, "If they buy it, we will print it." But it is clear that the
conflict between the subject matter he thinks the press should
pursue and the institutional need to balance the bottom line no
longer exists.

One of the better-known public examples of this kind of
conversion resulted from the pilgrimage of Malcolm X to Mecca
shortly before his death. As a follower of Elijah Muhammad's ver-
sion of the Muslim religion, Malcolm X was a black separatist who
believed that all white people were evil. His experience in the
Muslim world caused him to reconsider these fundamental convictions. He wrote a letter to his assistants in the United States, which
he asked them to duplicate and distribute to the press, in which he
recounted his experiences in Mecca and his responses to them. A
passage from that letter describes his changing beliefs:

> There were tens of thousands of pilgrims from all over the world.
> They were of all colors, from blue-eyed blondes to black-skinned Af-
> ricans. But we were all participating in the same ritual, displaying a
> spirit of unity and brotherhood that my experiences in America had
> led me to believe never could exist between the white and the
> non-white. . . .
> You may be shocked by these words coming from me. But on
> this pilgrimage, what I have seen, and experienced, has forced me
> to *re-arrange* much of my thought-patterns previously held, and to
> *toss aside* some of my previous conclusions. This was not too diffi-
> cult for me. Despite my firm convictions, I have been always a man

who tries to face facts, and to accept the reality of life as new experience and new knowledge unfolds it. I have always kept an open mind, which is necessary to the flexibility that must go hand in hand with every form of intelligent search for truth.[1]

A difference of opinion could exist as to whether Malcolm X was encountering a new face of the Islam religion of which he was already an adherent, or whether his experience was that of entering a new institutional context, a different Muslim religion. In either case, his response is the same for our purposes. When he encountered an institutional expectation about the treatment of white people, he converted. In his words, "In the past, yes, I have made sweeping indictments of *all* white people. I will never be guilty of that again—as I know now that some white people *are* truly sincere, and that some truly are capable of being brotherly toward a black man. The true Islam has shown me that a blanket indictment of all white people is as wrong as when whites make blanket indictments against blacks."[2]

Conversions are not always as sudden or as dramatic as the one described by Malcolm X. They do not always fit cleanly into the typology of a single conflict between a person's own agenda and an institution's agenda that results in a clear decision in favor of the latter. The transformation of personal agendas can be a matter of evolution, taking place slowly as an individual repeatedly confronts contrary expectations in a variety of institutional settings. Such as the case in the life of Eleanor Roosevelt, as recounted by Blanche Wiesen Cook.

Eleanor Roosevelt was born into a family milieu that valued privilege, social and racial hierarchy, rigid gender stereotypes, and a triumphalist nationalism. Over the course of her life she faced repeated challenges to the patrician agenda that she had accepted as her own as she moved through a variety of corporate contexts, including boarding school and later association with labor organizers, feminists, peace activists, and political groups with alternative visions of the public good. As a result, she became a major defender of a liberal democratic, indeed occasionally a radical, political agenda. This change, however, was not an immediate response to this alternative vision:

> Her commitment to a life of engaged political action involved the most pressing and controversial issues of the twentieth century:

women and power, race and class, war and peace; issues of justice, economic security and human rights. Her views changed slowly over time. She became an antiracist activist, although she began her public career steeped in the sensibilities of the Old South, filled with distorted and ugly images of blacks and Jews. The distance she traveled on issues of race, gender, and class, her ability to stand up for what she believed, involved conscious struggle.[3]

She succeeded in this deliberate, conscious struggle to move away from her old agenda and embrace a new one to the point that Secretary of State John Foster Dulles once called her "more subversive and dangerous than Moscow."[4]

External observers will view such conversions differently, often depending on whether they agree or disagree with the content on the newly embraced agenda. "Selling out" is a label that is sometimes attached to those one-time youthful radicals or liberals who change their political stripes as they move into the business world, professional careers, or other institutions of the establishment. Some people complain to friends who had been community activists that they have been co-opted by the prestige or other trappings of political institutions as their political agendas change with success.

Those who choose the convert's response may also have to reckon with charges that they are fickle, weak, or unprincipled. Presidents George Bush and Bill Clinton have both had to respond to these kinds of charges when they have departed from what seemed to be a personally valued agenda to a different one championed by others in the institution of government. Malcolm X disillusioned some followers who complained, "He doesn't know *what* he believes in. No sooner do you hear one thing than he's switched to something else."[5] An individual who wants others to take his values and beliefs seriously needs to demonstrate to others that he takes them seriously himself.

No doubt such negative assessments of changes in agendas are justified at times. But conversions can also rightly be characterized by such terms as *growth* and *maturation*. It would be the height of arrogance to believe, at any given point in time, that any one of us has all of the right answers. Surely we can continue to learn from others, a continuing education that encompasses not only facts but also values. And the way we learn from others is through social interaction, in groups and communities. The institution is the medium through which we can come to understand and appreciate other points of view.

When we think about persons as social selves[6] we are reminded that each self comes into existence only in the midst of institutions. Everything that we know and all of the values that we affirm come to us through interaction with others in institutional contexts. Personal agendas are created by our appropriation from institutional agendas. While we will inevitably experience conflict between personal and institutional agendas from time to time, personal agendas that make such conflict possible exist because we have previously accepted and embraced other institutional expectations as our own.

So personal agendas have been created in the first place only because we have, at times, chosen the convert's response to institutional agendas. And, on a continuing basis, personal agendas change through a similar process. Our personal morality evolves when we claim for ourselves the values and expectations that have been given to us by others. For some social institutions—such as schools, religious groups, and political parties—shaping or forming personal agendas constitutes a major reason for their existence.

A clarification: Our image of a person's responding to conflicting agendas should not be one of an independent, autonomous self standing apart from institutions and judging their agendas. Rather, we could think about a conflict between agendas as a conflict between institutional agendas: the institutional agenda the individual previously converted to and now affirms as her own, and the institutional agenda that is currently presenting a contrary expectation. Each time an individual chooses the convert's response, the process of refining personal morality continues.

The response of John, as a convert, to the country club issue is fairly clear. While not automatically deferring to the authority of the club in the way that the institutionalized person does, the result is the same. After examining the values entailed in the conflict, John accepts the club's expectations as his own. He could reject his personal belief that persons should be treated equally regardless of race, or he could decide that his understanding of the meaning of that belief that led him to think there was a conflict in agendas was mistaken. A wholesale rejection of his belief in equal treatment could come through a recognition that the club's members believe that there are meaningful differences between whites and African Americans, that they expect discriminatory choices to be made on that basis, and John decides that such a view is correct. In this instance, John simply ceases to believe that people should be treated equally.

His reasoning could be more subtle, leading him not so much to abandon the idea of equal treatment as to reject the meaning he had attached to that idea. He might focus on legitimate expectations of privacy and freedom of association, taking an approach something like the following: This is a private club. It is supported by voluntary, individual contributions. People should be able to form such close associations with whomever they wish. (After all, don't African Americans have their own groups that exclude whites?) Club membership is not some public good such as employment or education or health care that is being denied to others. Throughout our lives we constantly, in fact we must, draw boundaries between those with whom we will associate on a personal, intimate basis, and those with whom we can relate on only a more distant basis. Nonwhites are not being excluded from the club by any formal policy. Even if the cumulative effect of the individual choices of members is to perpetuate a homogeneous membership, no one is being denied anything to which they are entitled. John would conclude from this kind of reasoning that he was wrong in his interpretation of the meaning of equal treatment that led him to think there was a conflict of values here.

Whether John deletes the equal treatment item from his personal agenda, or radically reinterprets its meaning so that it is no longer the same value, the conversion has taken place. He does not experience the lingering guilt of the improvisor; he does not feel that he has settled for the arbitrator's half-way measures or resigned himself to the pluralist's powerlessness. He has become convinced that the institution's values were better than his and he has willingly made the switch. While occasional conversions are a sign of life in any individual, conversions that are too drastic and too frequent are a sign that one's personal center has been lost.

Part III

Choosing an Agenda

10

The Response Ethic of a Social Self

In parts 1 and 2, I have described an ethics of response, discussed how the concept of the agenda can serve as a metaphor for the way we encounter moral expectations, and developed a typology of responses that are available to us as we respond to conflicting agendas. The next obvious questions are: If individuals do face the value conflicts I have described, and if they do have these kinds of options to choose among, how should they choose? In any particular situation, how does a person know which response is appropriate? How should an individual think about the available alternatives? The purpose of this chapter is to draw together some thoughts about a response ethic and the image of responding to agendas in order to offer some general observations about choosing among the types of responses that have been presented. These general observations lay the groundwork for the more specific advice and comments that follow in the next chapter.

Writing about a person's choice of responses to institutional agendas is a tricky matter. Not only are a person's responses to institutional agendas influenced by those institutions, but the very person, the self, that is making the choices is a creation of social institutions. This notion of the self as socially constructed is, however, at the core of an ethics of response. The person making the ethical response is viewed not as a bystander or external observer of social activity but as a person immersed in that activity, an immersion not of a discrete entity but of a person that is an inseparable part of the continuing interaction of beings.

To be a self is to exist in relation to other selves, selves that constitute groups, that make up communities that form institutions. To be a self is to be a constitutive part of human institutions. Thus, when we encounter moral norms, mediated through institutional agendas, we encounter not a set of prescriptions coming from some external source but, in the words of H. Richard Niebuhr, "our own imperatives which we can disobey only at the cost of inner conflict and suffering, which we can deny only by giving up ourselves."[1]

This understanding of the self as a social self can be contrasted with some modern views of the individual that seem to start with a self that is independent, unencumbered, and autonomous. The concept of conscience, that inner voice directing an individual's moral action, can be thought of as the anchor of the autonomous self's ethical decision-making capacity. Searching one's conscience is often presented as an individualistic, private alternative to accepting the judgment of others. For Niebuhr this is a social event. Even conscience itself is enmeshed in social relationship: "The experience of conscience is not *like* being judged by another person; it is indeed being judged by another, though the other is not immediately or symbolically and physically present to the sense-experiencing man. Conscience is a function of my existence as a social being, always aware of the approvals and disapprovals of my action by my fellow men." We come into being only in relationship to others. To say that I am I is to acknowledge my existence as a counterpart to other selves. The self is fundamentally social in the sense that it not only knows itself in relationship to other selves, but exists only in those relationships.[2]

The observers of American life who wrote *Habits of the Heart* are aware of the importance of relationships, of social and historical context, of not forgetting what we have received from others: "We find ourselves not independently of other people and institutions but through them. We never get to the bottom of ourselves on our own. . . . All of our activity goes on in relationships, groups, associations, and communities ordered by institutional structures and interpreted by cultural patterns of meaning." But these observers are also aware of the importance of avoiding the extreme understanding, based on socialization and conditioning, that concludes that there is no self at all, that "what seems to be a self is merely a series of social masks that change with each successive situation."[3] Thus, as we noted earlier, the social self encompasses both a social "me" and a creative "I." The companionship of fellow knowers is important, but so is the reality of direct personal experience that is not simply derivative of the group.[4] Any observations about the choice of response to conflicting agendas should take into account both realities—persons construct their social context and are constructed by it.

As we understand the significance of social context for a response ethics, we should also keep in mind Niebuhr's admonition that we not conceive of our social context too narrowly: "[O]ur life in response to action upon us, our life in anticipation of response to our reactions, takes place within a society whose boundaries cannot be drawn in space, or time, or extent of interaction, short of a whole in which we live and move and have our being. The responsible self is driven as it were by the movement of the social process to respond and be accountable in nothing less than a universal community."[5] The preceding description of the self that responds to conflicting agendas gives us some clues about how choices should be made. These clues do not yield an approved set of rules to apply or a hierarchy of goals arranged in order of priority. They do, rather, give us some insight into the ethical task at hand and suggest how we should proceed to choose among the available options. Our struggle to find appropriate responses to the conflicts between personal and institutional agendas should be marked by three elements: (1) continuing inquiry, (2) communal interaction, and (3) authenticity in response.[6]

The first premise is that the search for answers is never over. The point of view of any person is always limited, partial, finite. We have come to be and to know in particular places and in particular times. Therefore, we should always be open to new possibilities when we confront an ethical challenge. We should seek to make appropriate responses with a willingness to learn, to discover new and different truths, to be enlightened by different perspectives.

The continuing inquiry is more than a search for new information. It is also an openness to new ways of interpreting and evaluating the world we are learning about. This kind of flexibility takes us into our encounters with institutions with no final rules, with no fixed goals. We are called to a humility that admits that there are things we do not know and conclusions that we may have to change. Our response comes in an ongoing conversation that continually promises new experiences, perspectives, and answers.

The second feature of our search for appropriate responses is communal interaction. We do not engage in this continuing inquiry as a solitary self, but as a member of communities. Obviously it is only with the aid of others that we broaden our horizons and explore new worlds. Even more important, though, is the understanding that we are not simply the recipients of information sent to us by others. Ours is a relational inquiry in which the seeker is changed. This is not a one-way street. The continuing inquiry leads not only to our transforming the world but also to our being transformed by it. Choosing appropriate responses is not a matter of exerting control over an inert world, but of participating in a mutual, interactive relationship.

As an active participant in community, we are available to others for challenge, critique, and illumination—and for celebration. We give up our illusions of "self-made" individuals and explore, analyze, and rejoice in the relationships that make us what we are. We acknowledge our debts to our life companions and expect that our achievements will be proportional not to our success as solitary workers but to our success as responsive collaborators.[7]

These first two elements grow out of the understanding of the social self that stresses the social "me," the aspect of the self that is formed by others. As such, the emphasis is on the incompleteness of the self and its reliance on others, the way one's context shapes and molds her values and knowledge. The understanding of the social self described above, however, also affirms an aspect of individuals that is not wholly derivative of one's context, and thus we add a third feature to the search for appropriate responses: authenticity.

We speak of persons making authentic responses because we have some sense of a personal integrity that allows an individual's response to be something more than mimicry. We can conceive of persons as actively interdependent, rather than passively dependent. The authenticity of one's response is rooted in that person's identity as a creative "I" that is not reducible to the social influences that have affected him. An authentic response is one in which a person is, after all else is said and done, true to herself.

Parker Palmer is writing about this kind of authenticity as he describes instances when individuals make an inner choice to stop leading "divided lives."[8] An example he cites of such personal wholeness is Rosa Parks making a decision not because she wanted to start a civil rights movement but simply because her feet were tired. This kind of choice comes when one is not willing to be something different on the outside than on the inside. The primary reference for such a response is a person's own sense of who she is. In the days when the Iron Curtain still stood, Vaclav Havel wrote a critical, public letter to the chief Communist official in Czechoslovakia. He was later asked if he wrote the letter to start a revolution. His response was no, that he had written the letter to keep from committing suicide.[9]

Authentic responses are those that are concerned first with being faithful to oneself: no more collaboration with an oppressive system, no more conspiring in your own diminishment. These responses come when one is in touch with and acts out of that core of the self that escapes confinement by sociological explanation. Authenticity does not rule out cooperation with institutions, but it does entail a cooperation that comes as a person asks questions about the proper objects and scope of his loyalty and trust. An authentic cooperation is a consent, rather than a resignation, a consent that one gives when persuaded that there is value in an institution's symbols, and is moved to participate in that community.[10]

The congruence of this understanding of a response ethic and the image of the agenda can be seen by focusing on these three features of continuing inquiry, communal interaction, and authentic response. An agenda is a call for a response in an ongoing inquiry. It announces that additional deliberation and discussion are warranted. Further, an agenda is a call that establishes (or reaffirms) a community that is continuing a search for answers to identified problems or questions. By its very nature, an agenda reflects and anticipates community interaction on identified topics.

Finally, agendas are a call for a person's response in that ongoing conversation. They mark a continuing inquiry by the group, but they ask for an considered judgment by each individual. One cannot be a meaningful participant in such a discussion unless she brings something of herself to the conversation. A genuine personal response to an agenda comes from one who is not merely derivative of the institution but adds something of herself to the group.

The model that emerges for choosing among conflicting agendas is that of an authentic response in an ongoing conversation

with others. Such a model may be frustrating for those who want
the certitude of fixed unambiguous rules or a hierarchy of specified
ends. While more directive moral theories might impose more
order in the decision-making process, it is an artificial order that
obscures the complexity and particularity of moral life. For an
ethics of response, the decision-maker is left to rely on ideas of
moral intuition, seasoned judgment, sensitive imagination, and the
like.

James Gustafson's term for this process is moral discernment. This sophisticated concept cannot be fairly summarized
here. We can note that his understanding of moral discernment
brings to mind important features of an ethics of response that have
been mentioned earlier: an evaluative description of the occasion
or circumstances that prompt ethical reflection; the decision-maker's particular social location and perspective; the values, affectiv-
ities, and dispositions of the responder; and a rational, reflective
activity tested by others. Such ingredients yield an understanding
of the way we approach the task of choosing the appropriate response to conflicting agendas: "The final discernment is an informed intuition; it is not the conclusion of a formally logical argument, a strict deduction from a single moral principle, or an
absolutely certain result from the exercises of human 'reason'
alone. There is a final moment of perception that sees the parts in
relation to a whole, expresses sensibilities as well as reasoning, and
is made in the conditions of human finitude. In complex circumstances it is not without risk."[11]

How do I test my responses to competing claims? The
paradox is that I test my responses to institutions through reference
to institutions. Our values emerge and are validated in a community of selves. There is a circularity of the process. We are engaged
in a never-ending project of moving back and forth between personal, particular judgments and communal understandings of appropriate behavior—constantly checking one against the other.
Sometimes our personal judgment will lead us to reassess the community's standards; sometimes the process will be reversed. In
each case we will be called to fashion an authentic response in our
continuing conversation with others.

11

Making the Appropriate Response

This concluding section presents a series of more concrete observations about making personal responses to institutional agendas. The first four observations say something about the way we encounter agendas and how they function in our lives. These are primarily descriptive. The remaining comments are more prescriptive, offering some advice about how we should respond to institutional expectations.

We can't live our lives in isolation from institutional agendas.

There are limits to the extent we can be "hermits." We can avoid becoming part of particular institutions and can renounce our membership in others. But only in the rarest, most extreme cases can we live our lives outside of all institutions. When we rebel against social institutions, renouncing their agendas and terminating our memberships, we usually do so through reliance on the agendas of other institutions. The people in our society who live "on the margin" have not isolated themselves from all institutional agendas. Rather, they have traded in their memberships in mainstream groups for those that are typically smaller, less formal, less demanding, less rigid in presenting expectations and more in tune with their personal agendas.

We are social creatures. It is an illusion to think that our personal agendas are ever solely our own creations. Even a person's commitment to the individualistic notion of "being his own man" is one that has been forged and continually reinforced through a matrix of familial, educational, religious, and social institutions. Beyond this observation that personal agendas are shaped by institutional expectations is the reality that most of us rely on the cooperation or support of others to meet many of our needs: income (which translates into food, clothing, shelter), education, religious development and guidance, achievement of social goals, collegial respect, nurture and love. This cooperation and support comes to us through groups and institutions that establish expectations of us in the enterprise.

Therefore, when thinking about our responses to institutional agendas, very few of us have the choice of really opting out, of ignoring all group expectations in the pursuit of our personal agenda. We will inevitably be outside of some institutions as we seek others that are more compatible with our own sense of what is appropriate. Indeed, communal support, within one group or another, is often vital to one's ability to swim against an institutional stream. Our task will thus normally be picking and choosing among institutional agendas that will affect our lives, not avoiding them completely.

Institutional agendas can be life-giving and death-dealing.

Try to imagine your life as one in which all of your moral decisions were made without the shaping influence of institutional expectations. In such a life, each and every choice would be made without regard for what was expected of you by family members, colleagues, teachers, religious leaders, government officials (including the police), or fellow workers (including bosses). You would make no effort to anticipate the responses to your actions of those who mediate institutional expectations; there would be no sense of accountability to these others.

The first adjective that comes to mind when I imagine such a life is *chaotic.* The second is *paralyzed.* The vision I have is one of gridlock, a situation in which a virtually infinite number of facts and values arrive at my mind's entrance, and I am left without an adequate mechanism to process them. Institutional agendas give form to what would otherwise be a chaotic life. They provide a structure, a way of interpreting, ordering, and responding to the incessant flow of life around us. They help us sort out the important from the unimportant, the causes I can take on from those that are beyond my reach, the matters to which I should give serious attention out of the many that I cannot. These agendas provide a bulwark that keeps the self from being overwhelmed.

In this sense, these sets of expectations are life-giving. They give us the means to live in the midst of what would otherwise be chaos. If every decision had to be made on our own, if we did not rely on the benchmarks and guidance provided by the agendas of the groups to which we belong, we would have neither the time nor energy (not to mention wisdom) to order our lives in a meaningful way.

Agendas can also be death-dealing. The danger posed by institutional agendas is that our lives will become overly structured, that these expectations will become a stifling, oppressive presence that will snuff out the sparks of creativity and individuality that distinguish each of us from our environment. When this occurs, institutional agendas become stultifying. Instead of serving the quest for personal aspirations, they reduce lives to the lowest common denominator, inevitably resulting in unfulfilled lives and unrealized possibilities. Life is often best found in an acceptance of the transience of any particular state of affairs. As long as we view ourselves as temporary guests in our institutional settings, we avoid becoming too settled, too content. We can keep distant from the mental, spiritual, and emotional death that comes with a conviction that we have found our final resting place.

So many of the forms, rituals, and ceremonies that are a part of our environment are attempts to capture life. These events—whether religious, civic, familial, or communal—are efforts to give meaning to our existence, to erect barricades against chaos and transience. These very barricades, however, can confine and kill. The form itself, meant to sustain life, can bring death. Rather than preserving our selves and bolstering our identities, these institutional trappings can create a process in which our identity as selves is molded into the institutional body.

A golden mean does not exist by which we can automatically draw some line indicating where an institutional agenda moves from life-giving to death-dealing. Each of us faces this personal challenge, the never-ending task of assessing the direction group expectations are taking us. The reality that we cannot live in isolation from institutional agendas is, in itself, not troubling. The reality that these agendas can consume us is reason for constant vigilance as we respond to the communities of which we are a part.

Our responses are grounded in fundamental worldviews.

Everybody has a worldview. Everybody views the world from a particular perspective that is, at bottom, based on something like fundamental religious beliefs—beliefs about human beings and nature and history. Such beliefs form the elements of a meaning system through which we grasp the world, order our experience, and understand our existence. These basic assumptions are often taken for granted, but they exert a powerful influence on the way we interpret and respond to our universe. We cannot follow every agenda, and we must make decisions about priorities for the few we do embrace. These decisions are undergirded by our worldviews. When we respond to agendas, when we decide who counts and what matters, we do so as individuals who are viewing the world from a particular vantage point. Our choices will be *our* choices because they grow out of our own peculiar slant on reality.

A specific element in the approach to morality presented earlier is answering the question, "What's going on?" Determining what is going on, however, is more than noting specific words that are spoken or observing the movement of physical bodies. A meaningful analysis of what's going on will entail interpretation of such actions, and the answer will vary depending on whether we believe what's *really* going on is, to mention a few examples: the work of an ultimate power to redeem history; an endless cycle of death and rebirth; a finally meaningless passing of biological organisms; or the movement of humankind to higher levels of communal relationship.

The model of following agendas places more confidence in the exercise of an intuitive moral sense than do approaches which stress obedience to received rules or pursuit of chosen goals. This exercise of moral judgment is inevitably and profoundly affected by the beliefs, held consciously or unconsciously, that constitute the worldview of the decision-maker. When agenda conflicts arise, they can often be understood only through a serious examination of the different worlds of meaning that are operative in the situation.

Agendas begin discussions rather than end debates.

In chapter 2, we explored the approach to moral decision making that is suggested by the concept of the agenda. As noted there, putting an item on an agenda is more like beginning a discussion than ending a debate. Agenda setting is the process of communicating expectations through identifying who counts, what matters, and the context in which the people who count deal with the issues that matter. This process has a different flavor than the processes that dictate which goals are to be achieved or which rules are to be obeyed.

There are, of course, those situations in which the shaping of an agenda appears to control the outcome. There are meetings in which the adoption of an agenda is hotly debated and the decision in fact closes the discussion. In such cases it seems that the public act of agenda setting is the acting out of private and hidden agendas that were previously adopted. Vigorous debates about public agendas flow from conflicting views that have already been established (beyond public view) about desired actions.

A model of responding to public agendas has the potential, at least in the early stages of conversation, for promoting a less contentious exchange between persons with conflicting agendas. It is less confrontational to take the position that a particular course of action does not fit my personal agenda than to take the position that that particular course of action is wrong in some absolute, objective sense. While avoiding confrontation may not always be possible or desirable, there does seem to be considerable benefit in a model that alters our conversations about moral choices in ways that encourage an exchange of viewpoints, that offers possibilities for building relationships rather than erecting barriers between people. Dialogue is, indeed, "the primary means of preventing and resolving conflict."[1]

A key ingredient, then, of agenda setting is the creation of conditions for discourse, avoiding (when possible) strident divisions that force people away from one another. A model for this kind of approach to conflict is provided by Lisa Sowle Cahill in her description of public policy discourse as a commitment to civil exchanges among varying traditions.[2] This stance of dialogue and openness involves communities that challenge dominant values not by standing over against the larger group but by participating in it. The emphasis on a consensual mode of discourse and mutual critique is consistent with a call for "freedom that does not entail isolation and community that does not enforce uniformity."[3]

Once I have concluded that a course of action doesn't fit my personal agenda, an ensuing conversation may well bear on the kind of judgment I think others should make. The reasons I give for my choice could well imply that their agenda should change or that, in my view, the particular course of action is not appropriate within their agenda either. But the character of this exchange is different from one which begins with a declaration that a certain course of behavior is wrong and those who take it are blameworthy—especially if the other person has already engaged in that behavior.

In the end, choosing a different agenda and making different choices in light of that chosen agenda will be seen by some as rejection of their values. When I was considering a job change, I was given some firm advice by a friend and senior colleague: don't make a lateral move in your mid-thirties. His reasons were that my vocational advancement would be hampered, that the new position was a dead-end with no attractive step beyond it. I don't think that it ever registered with him that I did not have a vocational agenda that was dominated by a career ladder. My focus was on doing things I wanted to do with people I wanted to do them with. I received his advice, then took the new job. My colleague may have felt some rejection by my decision, but I'm certain there was less insult taken than if I had expressed a view that his approach to vocational agendas was inherently flawed and he was at fault for taking such a position.

Such an example is trivial, of course, in light of differences that arise over such issues as economic oppression, racial injustice, and environmental preservation. The way personal choices are made regarding even such potentially explosive issues as these is affected by a consideration of the reality that different people encounter different sets of expectations. It is understandable that different responses may be appropriate for persons acting in different contexts and in the midst of different communities. The image of responding to agendas readily allows for an understanding that others, striving to live good lives, may choose to follow other agendas that are grounded in traditions that we can recognize without accepting them as our own.

We should strive to respond to agendas in ways that keep the conversation going.

Following the observation that agendas begin discussions, I want to suggest that we should try to keep those discussions going in the way we respond to institutional agendas. In the pluralistic world of the end of the twentieth century, we are without a commonly acknowledged basis for making ethical choices. The moral and religious diversity that characterizes our world leaves us without an appeal to universally accepted authorities or principles. There appears to be no established way in our society of deciding between contradictory moral claims.[4]

In the midst of such diversity, continuing the discussion of our values and norms, of our varying agendas, is essential. The question is not whether there will be public conversations involving morality, but how intelligent, searching, and open those conversations will be.[5] We will not always reach agreement in such conversations, but the character of our life together will be profoundly affected by the mutual respect that should be reflected in these discussions.

Listening to others does not require that we give up or that we abandon our own point of view. But listening, really listening, does entail an openness to self-discovery and to new discoveries about others and their positions. What is called for is an acknowledgment that all of our truths are partial, that all of our understandings are incomplete, that we are always in process. This kind of acknowledgement means that we may learn something in the continuing conversation. Making others more like us is not the only reason for interacting with them.

This notion of mutual respect through continuing discourse can be at risk in several of the response types described in part 2. Respect for those who are the guardians of an institutional agenda does not prohibit one from being a reformer, but it does inform the way reform is attempted. It seems that one reason for Martin Luther King's insistence on nonviolent methods was precisely this concern that conversations continue even in the midst of reform efforts: "[Violence] is immoral because it seeks to humiliate the opponent rather than win his understanding; it seeks to annihilate rather than to convert. Violence is immoral because it thrives on hatred rather than love. It destroys community and makes brotherhood impossible. It leaves society in monologue rather than dialogue."[6] When the combination of intolerable institutional agendas and commitment to personal agendas leads one into the reformer's response, that response can still be fashioned with a concern that relationships be continued, that conversations not cease.

The other response that flows from the combination of intolerable institutional agendas and a commitment to personal agendas is that of the hermit. Here, too, there is a place for contributing to a continuing discussion. It is true, of course, that one can simply pack her bags and leave—disappear, terminating the institutional membership without comment. One can also "exit with voice" by making a final contribution to an institution's conversation while leaving it. While such a "parting shot" may be easily dismissed by others, the act also provides the opportunity for igniting a new round of debate from which many parties could benefit. Indeed, the responsibility of having been a part of an institution may bear on how one leaves, such as in the case of the resignation of a public official: "[T]o resign in silence or with false reassurance to the public that there is nothing wrong may be the least ethically defensible course of all: the buying of a separate peace at the expense of the entire process of responsible government."[7]

Communication must flow both ways in genuine conversations, which means that those who represent the institution also have a responsibility to understand and respect the human value of the hermits and the reformers. I recall a *Doonesbury* comic strip in which a university president informs a group of alumni that student protests today have a different tone than those of the 1960s. The reader then sees a student in coat and tie, in front of a "Divestiture Now, Please" sign. The student is talking to a police officer: "And here's a list of those requesting arrest, sir." The police officer responds in kind: "Thanks, son. That's a big help."[8]

I would not attempt to begin to explain this comic. One reality it could illustrate is the possibility that protest, even unlawful protest, need not be implemented or received as a dehumanizing activity. There are many reasons why the student protests of the sixties did not follow the style in the Doonesbury strip. One of those reasons was that the institutional representatives were often unwilling to make a place for the reformist agendas in their conversations. Whether in families, religious organizations, or professional circles, the common cause is better served when reforming instincts are viewed by others within the institution as contributions to a dialogue rather than as personal threats.

There is also a place for mutual respect within the other types of personal responses to institutional agendas. The purveyors of the group's agenda should be sensitive to and concerned about the limits that the "split personality" has placed on the range of institutional dominance. Conversely, that person has a responsibility to communicate when that line is being crossed before the group discovers it has lost a member. "Institutionalized persons" should not be taken for granted by the group, and those persons have an obligation to speak up when a spark of new possibilities is glimpsed—even if it appears out of line with the institutional agenda of the moment. The "accommodator" is in the most precarious position of all. The kinds of compromises, sacrifices, and efforts at incremental improvement in which he engages can only be sustained over time if there is a willingness on all sides to acknowledge what is going on and why the effort is worthwhile.

Personal agendas must exclude some things. By its very nature, one's agenda cannot be everything, and there is a virtue in seeing beyond what comes with a particular agenda. While my agenda presents a limited vision of who counts and what matters, it is important to see that the agendas of others embrace other communities, issues, contexts. It is important in my conversations to show an awareness of and an appreciation for the agendas and choices of others. I will also hope that I will be the beneficiary of a similar respect and appreciation from them.

We should not fall into an agenda.

I do not want to reach age sixty-five (or seventy, or any other age) and look back at what I have done and regret that my life feels more like what happened to me than what I did. I want to be sure to force myself to make periodic reassessments of where I am and where I think I am going. In this way, I hope I can be sure that I will be looking back at decisions made by me, not for me; that I will be looking back on conscious, deliberate choices rather than natural evolutions, comfortable accommodations, and postponements of true engagement or struggle. Going one step further, I think it is important that agenda formation be an active process, not simply a passive reacting to whatever comes along. Our creation and recreation of personal agendas should be guided by some vision of the "the good," directed and sustained by fundamental values that we claim as our own.

One implication of striving to make intentional decisions

about agenda choices is the need to reflect on the agendas I am, in fact, following. How do we know what our priorities for agendas are? Many people say their jobs are not the most important things in their lives, but look at the energy and passion (not to mention the time) they put into them. What fuels our actions and commitments? Where do we get our motivation, our energy? All of us allow parts of our agendas to be set by others. It is important that we be engaged in an intentional negotiating process, aware of who determines how much of our agenda and why.

The desire not to fall into an agenda, or to accept automatically the agenda into which I was born, means that I don't want to default unreflectively into the pattern of the institutionalized person. With some hesitancy, I would also urge others not to assume that style without conscious deliberation. The hesitancy in steering others away from this choice reflects a sensitivity to the not-uncommon complaint from some people that they have "seen too much." Specific examples can be found among persons who have been engaged in the graduate study of religion. It is not unusual for these students to emerge from their years of critical analysis with a very different view of their religious faith than they had going in. But the human mind's capacity to uncover uncertainties, pose questions, and deconstruct existing worldviews seems to run well ahead of the capacity to create certainty, answer questions, and construct new, satisfactory worldviews. Not surprisingly, the survivors of advanced religious studies occasionally long, somewhat wistfully, for the simpler, easily accepted faith of their youth, a faith they know they can never recapture.

There is something reassuring and secure about unquestioned faith in a group's cause. Given the limited perspective that any one of us can have, the tendency to accept the wisdom of others is understandable. I recognize a paradoxical aspect to the advice not to "fall" into an agenda. Having once stepped outside the institution far enough to make a conscious decision about unqualified institutional loyalty, a person may find it very difficult ever to step back in the same way. The memory of past questioning has the continuing potential to resurrect doubt about that allegiance, especially if the institution's agenda or one's life circumstances change.

The institutionalized person's response raises one central question: To whom do you grant authority to set your agenda and judge your actions? If individuals do not retain some authority for themselves, then it is difficult to see how they could be acting responsibly in the sense described in chapter 2. We act responsibly as we critically interpret and respond to the events in our life, anticipating the response of others in our community to our actions. If our response comes unreflectively, however, if our response is a routinized, unthinking obedience to a set of institutional expectations, that response seems to be more akin to instinctive reflex actions than to the kinds of human activities we usually label as morally responsible.

A variety of factors should be taken into account in choosing a type of personal response to institutional agendas.

My understanding of how individuals respond to institutional agendas is not one that suggests that someone consider the types of responses presented in this book and choose one as the best guide for all future decision making. We will make different choices at different times and in different places and with varying degrees of self-conscious awareness. An individual will embrace different types of responses in different institutions. Those different choices should be guided by the consideration of a number of factors, some of which are more directly connected with some options in the typology of responses than others. Some of the factors to be considered are described in the following paragraphs.

The degree of conflict between the institutional agenda and the personal agenda. An appropriate response to a group's agenda should be informed by the amount of conflict between its expectations and one's personal agenda. The degree of conflict should be viewed in terms of both the breadth of the gap in competing expectations and the significance of the issues involved. Acquiescence may be fitting when diametrically opposed options are confronted on an insignificant matter, while rejection of the corporate agenda may be proper when only a slight difference exists between the personal and institutional agenda, but that difference represents a line that one simply cannot cross. Institutionalized persons experience no such conflict, while hermits typically experience the most. Possibilities for the reformer, the split personality, the accommodator, and the convert will vary according to the degree of conflict.

The certainty with which one has adopted a personal agenda. The depth of conviction will vary from one item on an individual agenda to another. Greater deference to institutional norms is expected in those instances in which personal conclusions have been tentative or preliminary. Such deference may be especially fitting when the individual feels she has an incomplete grasp of the facts or is unable to assess the probable outcome of various courses of action. The contrary will be the case, of course, when the actor is deeply committed to a personal agenda and believes she knows exactly what she is doing. This certainty in one's convictions is an essential ingredient for anyone choosing to accept the loss that accompanies the hermit's response or the risk and sacrifice that often await the reformer.

Loyalty to the institution. The nature of our institutional memberships varies dramatically from one group to another. We can walk away from some groups with barely a second thought. Other memberships are essential to our sense of self-identity. We enter into some institutions as a means to meet a specific, temporary need, expecting that association to be time-limited and nonbinding. Other institutional memberships are expected to last a lifetime—till death do us part. When our personal agenda runs afoul of a group's agenda, it is important to assess the degree of loyalty we feel toward that group. Just as greater commitment to one's personal agenda tips the balance of choice more toward individual values, greater loyalty to the institution will give increased weight to consideration of the group's expectations. Of course, such loyalty on the part of the institutionalized person is unquestioned. The balancing efforts of the split personality and the accommodator are premised on the belief that there is value in the institutional agenda that warrants efforts to work out a compromise.

The scope of institutional agendas. Individuals often must take into account not only their loyalty to an institution but the breadth of the claims an institution makes on them. The nature of corporate demands varies from setting to setting. This variation is often related to the place we occupy within an institution. Individuals at times decline opportunities to increase their involvement in an institution because they are unwilling to meet the greater expectations that will be placed on them. Thus, one might chose to be a church member, but not a church school teacher or a minister.

One might be willing to work in a neighborhood political caucus, but not run for public office.

Ideally, individuals would choose institutions and accept roles within those institutions that entail agendas with whose scope they were comfortable. Volunteers for military service would accept the extensive demands of the United States Army when making that commitment. Men and women would choose to have children with full appreciation of the added responsibilities of parenthood. Opportunities to become leaders and officers in various groups would be declined when such changes extended the scope of corporate agendas in unacceptable ways. Such choices, however, are not always made with an adequate understanding of their consequences. Further, personal agendas change and institutional agendas change. As a result, the fit (or lack thereof) between the actual range of the group's claims and the individual's perception of a proper range can be a key ingredient in addressing conflict. For example, the scope of an institution's agenda may be so broad that there is not enough room left for a split personality response that would carve out adequate space for one's personal agenda.

The institutional tolerance for personal agendas. The incompatibility between group and individual values may be greater or less than initially meets the eye. A closer examination of corporate expectations may reveal that stated policies are loosely enforced or ignored altogether. The expected pursuit of certain goals may often give way to other concerns more compatible with the personal agenda. General agenda items may be so general as to leave huge areas to personal discretion. Exceptions may be tolerated. In these kinds of circumstances, strategies may be available to the individual to reduce the apparent clash of expectations, particularly those of the accommodator.

On the other hand, the appearance of space to pursue one's own agenda may be illusory. The rhetoric of free choice may be undercut by intense peer pressure. Lofty ideals may be espoused for their public relations value and bear little resemblance to the norms that actually drive institutional decision making. The promise of personal latitude may give way to the reality of institutional control, leaving the individual with fewer options for responding to incompatible claims. Thus, a response to conflicting agendas should be informed by an investigation of the institutional agenda that is actually in force, an agenda that may vary from formal or public expectations.

The prospects and cost of reform. The reformer does not always engage in a cost-benefit analysis. On occasion, individuals simply take their stand, joining with Martin Luther in saying, "Here I stand, I can do no other."[9] More often, though, potential reformers do assess whether an attempt to bring about change will be worthwhile. That conclusion is reached by estimating the prospect for success and the cost of making the effort. The implications are obvious: the more receptive the environment is to change, the more likely it is that individuals will choose this option. More hostile contexts, those that are most resistant to change and that threaten to exact a high price from those who rock the boat, drive dissidents to consider other options.

The existence and attractiveness of alternatives. The way we respond to the agenda of one institution is affected by the availability of substitute institutions, or the feasibility and desirability of getting along without an institution like this one. Quitting a job is easier if comparable positions are readily available. Some civic and social organizations may be virtually interchangeable with others. Many people have discovered they can get along without exclusionary country clubs or political parties or the churches in which they were raised. If alternatives are attractive or not deemed necessary the hermit's exit is more of a possibility, the risks of becoming a reformer are less, and opportunities will exist to pursue accommodating strategies more aggressively.

Agenda choices should focus on process as well as product.

We can view agendas as establishing a process or as producing a result. The first view focuses on the intrinsic value of responding to expectations in particular ways. The feeling is that there is something of worth in the very act of following group or personal expectations, apart from the consequences that may result. The second view is a more instrumental approach to agendas, evaluating the worth of expectations in terms of the results that will be produced by following them.

Recessions teach us a lot about career expectations. In every line of work understandings exist about how one prepares himself for particular jobs. Many people, however, have played by the rules, have acquired the appropriate credentials, and still find that their careers are beyond their control. Especially in times of recession we witness vast numbers of people who have faithfully followed an agenda only to discover that the desired result—securing and retaining a job—has not followed. Men and women who have always worked find themselves without jobs; companies who have never laid off workers find it necessary to do so. There is no guarantee that adhering to this agenda will yield the expected product.

If one has made decisions based only on an anticipated product, a deep feeling of regret may follow. All of the time and energy spent pursuing that end would understandably be viewed as wasted. I've had several occasions to counsel young women and men who were considering entering doctoral programs in fields in the humanities. The last two decades have not been happy ones for recent graduates who were seeking the teaching positions that are supposed to follow the receipt of a Ph.D. My words of wisdom to these seekers of advice have been that they should probably enter a graduate program only if they could value that educational experience for itself, only if they believed it would be worthwhile even if they never found a vocational setting in which that degree was useful. They should focus on the worth of the process as well as the value of the hoped-for product.

We strike different balances between valuing the process or the product in different settings. I think there are dangers that should be avoided in allowing the product-orientation to rule our choices of agendas in certain areas of life—for example, in the parenting of children. On the other hand, much that we value in life can be ours only as some aspiration toward certain goals—such as financial solvency, athletic excellence, a clean house—affects our choices about such matters as working overtime, torturous training, or cleaning toilets. The point is not that we should be oblivious to possible consequences of our choices, but that our choices should not fall prey to the twin dangers of always allowing the ends to justify the means or of always living out of tomorrow. We cannot always control the ends that result from our actions; we do not know what tomorrow will bring. Moral decisions that rest only on uncontrollable and unknowable futures are destined to be unhappy ones.

Conclusion

Agendas and Personal Responsibility

One aspect of the model of responding to agendas that troubles me, as I have mentioned previously, is the apparent emphasis on what a person does rather than who she is. I want to avoid a conception of morality that stresses the *actions* one performs to the exclusion of the person's *character*. A discussion of how one decides among the options presented in this book must look to the persons making the choices.

The decisions we make and the way we make them should reflect our character, particularly as the choices are made in a considered, consistent fashion rather than on a haphazard, ad hoc basis. Different concepts that have been used to describe this style of choice include the following: "self-direction," the complex, difficult, fallible process through which the individual makes his choices based on reflection, understanding, and calm judgment; "conscience," whose preeminent duty is the achievement and maintenance of the personal integrity or self-identity of the individual actor; "integrity," characteristic of a person whose decisions derive consistently from a core of deeply held ideals, with real attention given to her possibly conflicting ideals; and "judgment," a complex faculty through which we achieve a coherence among conflicting values.[1]

The words used in these discussions are *consistency, coherence, authenticity, honor.* The notion is that our grappling with value conflicts should emerge from a centered self, from a person maintaining some ethical authenticity. Such a self is differentiated from his environment. He acts out of a worldview, as discussed above, that defines his world and his place in it. He is not reacting reflexively to whatever stimulus comes along, but has fashioned and is acting upon a personal agenda.

Thus, when responding to institutional expectations, the choices made should give evidence of, as well as preserve and enhance, one's sense of self. A core of our selves exists that arbitrates among the competing claims, that untangles and gives meaning to the innumerable discrete decisions we make as we continually move from one community to another. Personal integrity is especially important in a world in which large and complex institutions seem to be beyond our reach or influence. Even when we despair that we can't make a difference, we can still strive to be true to ourselves, faithful to the agenda of our own making.

Our task is not to settle on the right mode for responding to institutional agendas, but to do what is fitting in each new situation. The challenge to act appropriately in an ever-changing world is an ongoing challenge. We must continually reexamine what's going on, review our options, and reconsider our choices. We choose our agendas experimentally, then revise them in the light of experience. In the end, we don't prove which response type is right. When justifying our choice to others, justifying our choice to ourselves, or counseling others, the justification is a matter of validation, not verification. We can give the reasons that guide our decisions, but these are reasons by which we attempt to be persuasive about the appropriateness of our judgment, not reasons by which we establish the truth of our claim.

The aim is for the arguments supporting our decision to be strong, powerful, and convincing. The enterprise is more akin to selling a product than to scientific discovery; the mode is the art of rhetoric rather than the skill of logical deduction. On first impression, linking ethical argumentation and salesmanship may be objectionable, but that impression may be misguided. When we sell products we try to demonstrate that the products effectively meet a legitimate need or serve a useful purpose. The pitch is that, on balance, one is better off with the product than with the money that would be paid for it. People should buy products when acquiring them is a proper way to respond to a particular problem or difficulty. The selling process is one of convincing or persuading potential buyers that buying a product is appropriate in a given set of circumstances, just as making a moral argument is an attempt to persuade a listener that adhering to a particular moral prescription is the appropriate choice in a given set of circumstances.

People do, of course, engage in undesirable selling techniques, such as misrepresenting products or using manipulative advertising to create needs. People also use undesirable techniques in selling ethical positions as well. In both cases we evaluate whether the rhetoric being employed is better or worse. At the heart of the persuasive process is the identity and integrity of the person making the choices. Our responses to ethical arguments in general, and to institutional agendas in particular, must be judged in part by how well they fit with who we are.

This view of personal integrity and self-identity should not be understood in an overly privatized, individualistic way. My agenda embodies the values of those who have gone before me. My perceptions and interpretations have been formed in community, and I will benefit from a greater willingness to learn from the lives of others. My own agenda can only be enriched as I push to expand my view to see the understandings and values of larger and larger communities.

A key to moral decision making is not to reject the possibility that others contribute to the choices I make, but to be as clear as possible about *who* and *what* are shaping my agenda, how much influence they have been given in the process, and why. Personal integrity requires a critical awareness of the interplay of persons in the midst of communities and groups. Somewhere within each person is a core, whether we call it conscience or intuition or faith, that defines this person in the midst of others. The image I wish to close with is not the image of a personal agenda that we have, like a possession, but of the unique persons that we are, persons who are not simply derivative of institutional memberships.

Notes

Introduction: It's Everybody's Problem

1. This account of the Challenger disaster is taken from a case study prepared by Nicholas Carter for the Harvard Program in Ethics and the Professions, reprinted in *Ethics and Politics: Cases and Comments,* ed. Amy Gutmann and Dennis Thompson, 2d ed. (Chicago: Nelson-Hall Publishers, 1990), 117–28.

2. Amitai Etzioni, *The Moral Dimension: Toward a New Economics* (New York: The Free Press, 1988), 4.

3. Ibid., 5.

4. Alan Goldman, *The Moral Foundations of Professional Ethics* (Totowa, N.J.: Rowman and Littlefield, 1980). Goldman himself finds these assertions unconvincing in most cases.

5. Albert Flores, "Introduction: What Kind of Person Should a Professional Be?" in *Professional Ideals,* ed. Albert Flores (Belmont, Calif.: Wadsworth Publishing Co., 1988), 1.

6. Michael Davis, "Thinking Like an Engineer: The Place of a Code of Ethics in the Practice of a Profession," *Philosophy and Public Affairs* 20, no. 2 (1991): 154–55, 162.

7. See, for example, Michael Bayles, *Professional Ethics* (Belmont, Calif.: Wadsworth Publishing Co., 1981), 7–11; Paul F. Camenisch, "On Being a Professional, Morally Speaking," in *Moral Responsibility and the Professions,* ed. Bernard Baumrin and Benjamin Freedman (New York: Haven Publications, 1983), 42–61.

8. In reaching this conclusion, I am agreeing with Mike W. Martin in his exchange of essays with Benjamin Freedman: Freedman, "A Meta-Ethics for Professional Morality," *Ethics* 89, no. 1 (1978): 1–19; Martin, "Rights and the Meta-Ethics of Professional Morality," *Ethics* 91, no. 4 (1981): 619–25; Freedman, "What Really Makes Professional Morality Different: Response to Martin," *Ethics* 91, no. 4 (1981): 626–30; Martin,

"Professional and Ordinary Morality: A Reply to Freedman," *Ethics* 91, no. 4 (1981): 631–33.

9. David Little has used the phrase "duties of stations," rather than duties of role or duties of office, in a similar attempt to be inclusive of all the requirements and responsibilities of social life. "Duties of Station vs. Duties of Conscience: Are There Two Moralities?" in *Private and Public Ethics: Tensions Between Conscience and Institutional Responsibility,* ed. Donald G. Jones (New York: Edwin Mellen Press, 1978), 154 n. 1.

10. This more integrative view of human moral behavior finds traditional distinctions distracting, such as those made by Reinhold Niebuhr, stating that it is never possible to eliminate "certain irreconcilable elements in the two types of morality, internal and external, individual and social," in *Moral Man and Immoral Society* (New York: Charles Scribner's Sons, 1932), 258; and Charles Frankel, who claimed that "the morality appropriate to the performance of a social role, and the morality of small-scale, face-to-face relations are different," in "Morality and U.S. Foreign Policy," *World View* 18 (April 1975): 19. Such distinctions separate out pieces of the moral life that can often be better understood as integral parts of a whole.

11. See, for example, Dorothy Emmett, *Rules, Roles and Relations* (New York: St. Martin's Press, 1966).

12. Such a reformist view is spelled out in Robert N. Bellah, William M. Sullivan, Ann Swidler, and Steven M. Tipton, *The Good Society* (New York: Alfred A. Knopf, 1991).

13. Robert Merton, *Social Theory and Social Structure,* 3d ed. (New York: The Free Press, 1968), 194. Merton's pioneering typology focused on the contradictions in the cultural and social structure. The focus of the typology developed in this book is the contradictions between individual norms and institutional norms. The difference in focus yields a different kind of typology although there are points at which the two analyses meet.

1. Agendas

1. Formally, agenda is the plural form of agendum. Common practice will be followed here with "agenda" used as the singular and "agendas" as the plural form.

2. One study has concluded that a fundamental source of public dissatisfaction with the law may be individuals' pursuit of hidden agendas, resorting to the legal system in pursuit of objectives that are beyond the competence of the law and at odds with the operating assumptions of the legal system. John M. Conley and William M. O'Barr, "Hearing the Hidden Agenda: The Ethnographic Investigation of Procedure," *Law and Contemporary Problems* 51 (Autumn 1988): 181–97.

3. Milt Reitzfeld, "How to Deal with Expressive People," *Journal of Systems Management* 40 (January 1989): 21.

4. John W. Kingdom, *Agendas, Alternatives and Public Policies* (Boston: Little Brown and Co., 1984), 3–4.

5. Deborah Tannen, *You Just Don't Understand: Women and Men in Conversation* (New York: Ballantine Books, 1990), 33–37.

6. Roger W. Cobb and Charles D. Elder, *Participation in American Politics: The Dynamics of Agenda Building*, 2d ed. (Baltimore: John Hopkins Univ. Press, 1983), 86, 172.

7. Robert A. Heineman, William T. Bluhm, Steven A. Peterson, and Edward N. Kearny, *The World of the Policy Analyst: Rationality, Values, and Politics* (Chatham, N.J.: Chatham House Publishers, 1990), 58.

8. The process of putting an item on a formal institutional agenda is a complex one that has been most thoroughly studied in the political arena. See, for example, Keith J. Mueller, "The Role of Policy Analysis in Agenda Setting: Applications to the Problem of Indigent Health Care," *Policy Studies Journal* 16 (Spring 1988): 441–53; Jonathan Burden and Terry M. Moe, "Agenda Control, Committee Capture and the Dynamics of Institutional Politics," *American Political Science Review* 80 (December 1986): 1187–1207; Kingdom, *Agendas, Alternatives and Public Policies*; Nelson Polsby, *Political Innovation in America: The Politics of Policy Initiation* (New Haven, Conn.: Yale Univ. Press, 1984); Roger Cobb, Jennie-Keith Ross, and Marc Howard Ross, "Agenda Building as a Comparative Political Process," *American Political Science Review* 70 (March 1976): 126–38.

9. Peter L. Berger and Thomas Luckmann, *The Social Construction of Reality* (Garden City, N.Y.: Doubleday and Co., 1966), 61.

10. While this distinction has been given many expressions, a definitive formulation appears in George H. Mead, *Mind, Self, and Society* (Chicago: Univ. of Chicago Press, 1934), 173–200.

11. Jane Attanucci, "In Whose Terms: A New Perspective on Self, Role, and Relationship," in *Mapping the Moral Domain: A Contribution of Women's Thinking to Psychology and Education*, ed. Carol Gilligan, Janie Victoria Ward, and Jill McLean Taylor (Cambridge, Mass: Harvard Univ. Press, 1988), 201–24.

12. Gail Sheehy, *Passages: Predictable Crises of Adult Life* (New York: E. P. Dutton and Co., 1976).

2. Agendas and Ethical Reflection

1. H. Richard Niebuhr, *The Responsible Self: An Essay in Christian Moral Philosophy* (New York: Harper and Row, 1963). The description here of alternative views of human moral action draws significantly

from Niebuhr's discussion on pages 47–68 in which he develops his concept of man-the-answerer.

While the discussion of a response ethics in this book relies on the elements of an ethics of responsibility developed by Niebuhr, I have not in this project also drawn upon his theological convictions. Questions can always be asked about the appropriation of a method of analysis without including the subject of that analysis. At the core of Niebuhr's own thinking about ethics was a radical monotheism that affirmed that God is acting in all actions upon us and that we are called to respond to God's action. James Gustafson has commented concerning Niebuhr's ethics that "the method of responsiveness in ethics is, perhaps, as much a matter of seeing the ethical significance of that theological conviction as it is a matter of defining a type of ethics distinct from other historical types." ("Response to Francis Schussler Fiorenza," in *The Legacy of H. Richard Niebuhr*, ed. Ronald F. Thiemann (Minneapolis: Fortress Press, 1991), 75. I believe that there is value in Niebuhr's approach to ethics for those who do not necessarily share the substance of his theology, and the aim in this book as been to present this ethical methodology to that larger audience. My hope is that the loss in particularized meaning is offset in this presentation by the increased possibilities for appropriating the basic structure of an ethics of response.

2. Carol Gilligan, "Remapping the Moral Domain: New Images of Self in Relationship," in *Mapping the Moral Domain*, ed. Gilligan, Ward, and Taylor, 3–19.

3. William K. Frankena, *Ethics*, 2d ed. (Englewood Cliffs, N.J.: Prentice-Hall, Inc., 1973), 43–44.

4. Thomas E. Wartenberg, "Teaching Women Philosophy," *Teaching Philosophy* 11, no. 1 (1988): 19.

5. Niebuhr, *The Responsible Self*, 65.

6. The intuitive thesis that individuals act in response to the anticipated reactions of others is born out in different kinds of studies. One empirical study found that the propensity toward "ethical action" could decrease significantly "in a situation where one's actions would not be discovered by others"; John H. Barrett and Marvin J. Karson, "Personal Values and Business Decisions: An Exploratory Investigation," *Journal of Business Ethics* 6 (1987): 371–82. A game theoretic analysis by James Gaa focused on the relationship between the society at large and the professions that had been granted a certain autonomy by society in setting their own standards in exchange for serious efforts at self-policing. He found that the society's difficulty in ascertaining whether a profession is keeping the bargain increases the likelihood that the profession will lower its standards; James C. Gaa, "A Game-Theoretic Analysis of Professional Rights and Responsibilities," *Journal of Business Ethics* 9 (1990): 159–69.

7. A helpful description of how these four elements of Niebuhr's responsibility are analytically powerful in the context of business ethics can be found in James W. Kuhn and Donald W. Shriver, Jr., *Beyond Success: Corporations and Their Critics in the 1990s* (New York: Oxford Univ. Press, 1991), 286–93.

8. Aristotle, *Nicomachean Ethics,* trans. Martin Ostwald (Indianapolis: Bobbs-Merrill, 1962), 152–73.

9. Albert R. Jonsen and Stephen Toulmin, *The Abuse of Casuistry: A History of Moral Reasoning* (Berkeley: Univ. of California Press, 1988), 16–19.

10. Ibid., 18.

11. Carol Gilligan, *In a Different Voice: Psychological Theory and Women's Development* (Cambridge, Mass.: Harvard Univ. Press, 1982).

12. Some public choice theorists have asserted that in some situations group decisions *are* determined by the manipulation of the agenda. See, e.g., William H. Riker and Barry R. Weingast, "Constitutional Regulation of Legislative Choice: The Political Consequences of Judicial Deference to Legislators," *Virginia Law Review* 74 (1988): 385; and David P. Baron and John Ferejohn, "Bargaining and Agenda Formation in Legislatures," *The American Economic Review* 77 (May 1987): 303–9. In such situations the actual contesting of the outcome takes place at what could be called the pre-agenda stage: the discussion of the structure that will determine the structure for action, the bargaining that takes place in the agenda formation process.

13. Jonsen and Toulmin, *The Abuse of Casuistry,* 335.

14. Alasdair MacIntyre, *After Virtue,* 2d ed. (Notre Dame, Ind.: Univ. of Notre Dame Press, 1984), 204–12.

15. Eric Mount, Jr., *Professional Ethics in Context: Institutions, Images and Empathy* (Louisville, Ky.: Westminster/John Knox Press, 1990), 22.

16. For example, I have suggested an agenda for feminist husbands and fathers in Don Welch, *Macho Isn't Enough: Family Man in a Liberated World* (Atlanta: John Knox Press, 1985).

17. Michael Walzer, *Obligations: Essays on Disobedience, War, and Citizenship* (Cambridge, Mass.: Harvard Univ. Press, 1970).

18. Peter S. Wenz, *Environmental Justice* (Albany, N.Y.: State Univ. of New York Press, 1988), 316.

3. The Institutional Context

1. Karen McCarthy Brown points out that such conflict has been particularly acute and frequent for women and members of other low-

status groups whose agendas are not recognized as valuable and who find the content of institutional agendas being defined by an experience alien to their own. "Heretics and Pagans: Women in the Academic World," in *Private and Public Ethics,* 268–69.

2. Jeffrey Stout, *Ethics after Babel: The Language of Morals and Their Discontents* (Boston: Beacon Press, 1988), 289–91.

3. Anthony Giddens, *The Consequences of Modernity* (Stanford, Calif.: Stanford Univ. Press, 1990), 139.

4. Ibid., 90.

5. Albert Z. Carr, "Is Business Bluffing Ethical?" *Harvard Business Review* 46 (January-February 1968): 143–53.

6. Ibid., 145.

7. Emmett, *Rules, Roles and Relations,* 10.

8. Carr, "Is Business Bluffing Ethical?" 153.

9. Emmett, *Rules, Roles and Relations,* 50.

10. Carr, "Is Business Bluffing Ethical?" 148.

11. Quoted in Milton Snoeyenbos, Robert Almeder, and James Humber, eds., *Business Ethics: Corporate Values and Society* (Buffalo, N.Y.: Prometheus Books, 1983), 64.

12. Carr, "Is Business Bluffing Ethical?" 145.

13. James March and Johan P. Olsen, "The New Institutionalism: Organizational Factors in Political Life," *American Political Science Review* 78 (September 1984): 743.

14. Following Max Weber, power is understood here to be the opportunity to carry out one's own will, even against the resistance of others—regardless of the basis on which that opportunity rests. Authority is the *legitimate* exercise of carrying out one's will—legitimate in that it is seen by others as conduct grounded in recognized beliefs. Max Weber, *The Theory of Social and Economic Organization,* trans. A. M. Henderson and Talcott Parsons (New York: The Free Press, 1964), 152–53, 324–29.

15. H. R. Smith and Archie B. Carroll, "Organization Ethics: A Stacked Deck," *Journal of Business Ethics* 3 (1984): 95–100.

16. Dennis F. Thompson, *Political Ethics and Public Office* (Cambridge, Mass.: Harvard Univ. Press, 1987), 41–47.

4. The Hermit

1. James C. Thomson, Jr., "How Could Vietnam Happen? An Autopsy," *Atlantic Monthly* 221 (April 1968): 49.

2. *Public Utilities Commission v. Pollak,* 343 U.S. 451 (1952), 467.

3. William G. Scott and David K. Hart, *Organizational Values in America* (New Brunswick, N.J.: Transaction Publishers, 1989), 169.

4. Merton, *Social Theory and Social Structure,* 207.

5. Helen Rose Fuchs Ebaugh, *Becoming an Ex: The Process of Role Exit* (Chicago: Univ. of Chicago Press, 1988).

6. Zena Smith Blau first used the term *role exit* to identify this process in a paper, "Role Exit and Identity," delivered at the 1972 meeting of the American Sociological Association.

7. Henry David Thoreau, "Civil Disobedience," in *The Portable Thoreau,* ed. Carl Bode (New York: The Viking Press, 1947), 109, 131.

8. Thoreau, "Walden," in *The Portable Thoreau,* 324, 383, 290.

9. Thoreau, "Civil Disobedience," 131.

10. Thoreau, "Walden," 564–65.

11. Maggie Ross, *The Fire of Your Life* (New York: Paulist Press, 1983), 9, 34.

12. Maggie Ross, *Pillars of Flame: Power, Priesthood, and Spiritual Maturity* (San Francisco: Harper and Row, 1988), liv.

13. Ross, *The Fire of Your Life,* 135.

14. John Kekes, "Self-Direction: The Core of Ethical Individualism," in *Organizations and Ethical Individualism,* ed. Konstantin Kolenda (New York: Praeger Publishers, 1988), 15.

15. Carol Gilligan, "Exit-Voice Dilemmas in Adolescent Development," in *Mapping the Moral Domain,* ed. Gilligan, Ward, and Taylor, 142.

16. Ibid, 148.

17. Goldman, *The Moral Foundations of Professional Ethics,* 33.

5. The Institutionalized Person

1. Eric Hoffer, *The True Believer* (New York: Harper and Brothers, 1951), 61, 83.

2. Displayed at the General Store, Loretta Lynn's Dude Ranch, Hurricane Mills, Tennessee.

3. Scott and Hart, *Organizational Values in America,* 3.

4. John H. Fielder, "Organizational Loyalty," *Business and Professional Ethics Journal* 11 (Spring 1992): 72.

5. James R. Elkins, "Rites of Passage: Law Students 'Telling Their Lives,'" *Journal of Legal Education* 35 (March 1985): 43, 49.

6. Ross A. McDonald and Bart Victor, "Towards the Integration of Individual and Moral Agencies," *Business and Professional Ethics Journal* 7 (Fall-Winter 1988): 112–13.

7. Erich Fromm, *Escape From Freedom* (New York: Avon Books, 1941).

8. Bertolt Brecht, "The Measures Taken," trans. Elizabeth Hanunian, printed in Walzer, *Obligations,* 192.

9. Sidney Callahan, *In Good Conscience: Reason and Emotion in Moral Decision Making* (San Francisco: Harper San Francisco, 1991), 140.

10. Walzer, *Obligations,* 21.

11. Thoreau, "Civil Disobedience," in *The Portable Thoreau,* 112.

12. Rand and Dana Crowley Jack, *Moral Vision and Professional Decisions: The Changing Values of Women and Men Lawyers* (New York: Cambridge Univ. Press, 1989).

13. Lenore E. Walker, *The Battered Woman* (New York: Harper and Row, 1970), 45–52.

14. Ibid., 47.

15. Lenore E. Walker, *The Battered Woman Syndrome* (New York: Springer Publishing Co., 1984), 89.

16. Kathleen H. Hofeller, *Social, Psychological and Situational Factors in Wife Abuse* (Palo Alto, Calif.: R and E Research Associates, 1982), 123.

17. Merle Travis, "Sixteen Tons," © 1947 by Unichappell Music, Inc., and Elvis Presley Music (renewed). All rights on behalf of Elvis Presley Music administered by Unichappell Music, Inc. All rights reserved. Used by permission.

6. The Split Personality

1. Milton Friedman, "The Social Responsibility of Business is to Increase its Profit," in *Contemporary Issues in Business Ethics,* ed. Joseph R. Des Jordins and John J. McCall (2d ed.; Belmont, Calif.: Wadsworth Publishing Co., 1985), 9.

2. W. H. Walsh, "Pride, Shame and Responsibility," *The Philosophical Quarterly* 20 (January 1970): 7.

3. Herman Melville, *Billy Budd,* ed. F. Barron Freeman (Cambridge: Harvard Univ. Press, 1948).

4. Melville, *Billy Budd,* 239.

5. Max Weber, "Politics as a Vocation," in *From Max Weber,* ed. and trans. H. H. Gerth and C. Wright Mills (New York: Oxford Univ. Press, 1958), 95.

6. Walsh, "Pride, Shame and Responsibility," 7.

7. Albert Flores and Deborah G. Johnson, "Collective Responsibility and Professional Roles," *Ethics* 93, no. 3 (1983): 541.

8. See, for example, "Manifesto of the Communist Party," in Karl Marx and Fredrich Engels, *Basic Writings in Politics and Philosophy,* ed. by Lewis S. Feuer (Garden City, N.Y.: Doubleday & Co., 1959), 14–15.

9. Andrew Oldenquist, "Loyalties," *The Journal of Philosophy* 79 (April 1982): 187.

10. Sissela Bok, *Lying: Moral Choice in Public and Private Life* (New York: Random House, 1978), 258.

11. Lawrence Kohlberg and D. Candee, "The Relationship of Moral Judgment to Moral Action," in *Essays on Moral Development,* vol. 2, *The Psychology of Moral Development,* ed. Lawrence Kohlberg (San Francisco, Calif.: Harper and Row, 1984).

12. Edward Weisband and Thomas M. Franck, *Resignation in Protest: Political and Ethical Choices between Loyalty to Team and Loyalty to Conscience in American Public Life* (New York: Grossman Publishers, 1975), 1.

13. Gerald J. Postema, "Moral Responsibility in Professional Ethics," *New York University Law Review* 55 (April 1980): 64.

7. The Reformer

1. Martin Luther King, Jr., "I Have a Dream," in *The Great Society: A Sourcebook of Speeches,* ed. Glenn R. Capp (Belmont, Calif.: Dickenson Publishing Co., 1967), 86.

2. Michael Walzer, "Political Action: The Problem of Dirty Hands," *Philosophy and Public Affairs* 2, no. 2 (1973): 160–80.

3. Ibid., 166.

4. W. Kenneth Howard, "Must Public Hands Be Dirty?" *Journal of Value Inquiry* 11, no. 1 (1977): 39, 40.

5. Kenneth Blanchard and Norman Vincent Peale, *The Power of Ethical Management* (New York: William Morrow and Co., 1988), 7.

6. Max Weber, *The Protestant Ethic and the Spirit of Capitalism* (New York: Charles Scribner's Sons, 1958), 80.

7. Sissela Bok, "Whistleblowing and Professional Responsibilities," in *Ethics Teaching in Higher Education,* ed. Daniel Callahan and Sissela Bok (New York: Plenum Press, 1980), 280. Robert A. Larmer, however, argues that whistle blowing for moral reasons is acting in the employer's best interest and therefore involves no disloyalty. "Whistleblowing and Employee Loyalty," *Journal of Business Ethics* 11 (1992): 125–28.

8. Printed in Albert Flores, ed., *Ethical Problems in Engineering,* 2d ed., vol. 1 (Troy: Rensselaer Polytechnic Institute Press, 1980), 65–69.

9. Mike W. Martin, "Professional Autonomy and Employers' Authority," in *Profits and Professions: Essays in Business and Professional Ethics,* ed. Wade L. Robison, Michael S. Pritchard, and Joseph Ellin (Clifton, N.J.: Humana Press, 1983), 268.

10. *New York Times,* March 26, 1971, p. 53, col. 5.

11. James Boyd, "The Indispensable Informer," *The Nation* 228 (May 5, 1979): 497.

12. A case study of Dan Gellert's action is presented in Snoeyenbos, Almeder, and Humber, eds., *Business Ethics,* 282–86.

13. Ibid., 286.

14. Myron Peretz Glazer and Penina Migdal Glazer, "Individual

Ethics and Organizational Morality," in *Ethics, Government and Public Policy: A Reference Guide,* ed. James S. Bowman and Frederick A. Elliston (New York: Greenwood Press, 1988), 60–78. For an insightful look at the institution's case for mistreating whistle blowers and suggestions for how reform activities can be beneficially kept within channels, see Michael Davis, "Avoiding the Tragedy of Whistleblowing," *Business and Professional Ethics Journal* 8 (Winter 1989): 3–19.

15. Glazer and Glazer, "Individual Ethics," 69–70.

16. Natalie Dandekar, "Can Whistleblowing Be Fully Legitimated? A Theoretical Discussion," *Business and Professional Ethics Journal* 10 (Spring 1991): 97–98.

17. Albert O. Hirschman, *Exit, Voice and Loyalty: Responses to Decline in Firms, Organizations, and States* (Cambridge, Mass.: Harvard Univ. Press, 1970), 30, 83.

18. Ibid., 98.

19. Pierre Bourdieu, "An Antinomy in the Notion of Collective Protest," in *Development, Democracy and the Art of Trespassing: Essays in Honor of Albert O. Hirschman,* ed. Alegandro Foxley, Michael S. McPherson, and Guillermo O'Donnell (Notre Dame, Ind.: Univ. of Notre Dame Press, 1986), 301–2.

20. Martin Luther King, Jr., "Letter from Birmingham City Jail," reprinted in *Why We Can't Wait* (New York: Harper and Row, 1963), 159.

21. Scott and Hart, *Organizational Values in America,* 160.

22. Mount, *Profession Ethics in Context,* 75.

23. Reinhold Niebuhr, *Moral Man and Immoral Society* (New York: Charles Scribner's Sons, 1932), 277.

8. The Accommodator

1. Sullivan Ballou, Letter to Sarah Ballou, July 14, 1861. On file at the Illinois Historic Preservation Agency. Used by permission.

2. Gilligan, "Remapping the Moral Domain," 9. Gilligan credits Anne Glickman, the mother of the four-year-old boy, for the story.

3. J. Patrick Dobel, *Compromise and Political Action: Political Morality in Liberal and Democratic Life* (Totawa, N.J.: Rowman and Littlefield, 1990), 163–89.

4. See, for example, John C. Bennett, *Christian Ethics and Social Policy* (New York: Charles Scribner's Sons, 1956), 77–85.

5. Allan Gibbard, "Communities of Judgment," *Social Philosophy and Policy* 7, no. 1 (1989): 183.

6. Resolution adopted by Anti-Slavery Society, January 27, 1843.

7. David J. Fritzsch, "A Model of Decision-Making Incorporating Ethical Values," *Journal of Business Ethics* 10 (November 1991): 841–52, quote from p. 849.

8. Mary Catherine Bateson, *Composing a Life* (New York: Atlantic Monthly Press, 1989), 2–6, quote from p. 1.

9. Joseph Fletcher, *Situation Ethics: The New Morality* (Philadelphia: Westminster Press, 1966), 29.

10. R. N. Berki, "Machiavellism: A Philosophical Defense," *Ethics* 81 (January 1971): 124. As Berki notes, it is not that the politician has duties of a different kind but that she has less room to maneuver (p. 125).

11. Walzer, "Political Action: The Problem of Dirty Hands," 165–66.

12. Ibid., 166 (emphasis added in last sentence), 168.

13. Ibid, 171.

14. Jeremy Bentham, *The Principles of Morals and Legislation* (1789; rpt. New York: Hafner Publishing Co., 1948), 29–32.

15. An avowedly non-consequentialist approach to dissolving the dirty hands paradox is offered by Goldman, *The Moral Foundations of Professional Ethics.* Following this view the problem is not a problem because the apparent violation of a moral obligation is actually a case of one right or set of rights being properly overridden by stronger, more fundamental rights (p. 71).

16. The pure description of the calculator is embodied in the ethical theory of act utilitarianism. An approach that attempts to bridge this difference between the arbitrator and the calculator is rule-utilitarianism. See Frankena, *Ethics,* 34–43.

17. Mark Hansen, "P.D. Funding Struck Down," *ABA Journal,* May 1992, 18.

18. John Lachs, "'I Only Work Here': Mediation and Irresponsibility," in *Ethics, Free Enterprise, and Public Policy,* ed. Richard T. DeGeorge and Joseph A. Pilcher (New York: Oxford Univ. Press, 1978), 201–13.

19. Ibid., 205–6.

9. The Convert

1. *The Autobiography of Malcolm X* (New York: Ballantine Books, 1992), 390–91 (emphasis in original).

2. Ibid., 416.

3. Blanche Wiesen Cook, *Eleanor Roosevelt,* vol. I (New York: Penguin Books, 1992), 6.

4. Ibid., 19.

5. *The Autobiography of Malcolm X,* 482.

6. The concept of the social self is introduced in the section of chapter 2 on the shape of personal agendas and is discussed in more detail in chapter 10.

10. The Response Ethic of a Social Self

1. H. Richard Niebuhr, *The Meaning of Revelation* (New York: The Macmillan Co., 1941), 116.

2. Ibid., 75 (quote), 71.

3. Robert N. Bellah, Richard Madsen, William M. Sullivan, Ann Swidler, and Steven M. Tipton, *Habits of the Heart: Individualism and Commitment in American Life* (Berkeley: Univ. of California Press, 1985), 84, 80.

4. H. Richard Niebuhr, *Christ and Culture* (New York: Harper and Row, 1951), 245.

5. Niebuhr, *The Responsible Self,* 88.

6. I am indebted to Parker Palmer for suggesting this configuration of the basic elements of ethical decision making. Suggestions made at a workshop, Nashville, Tennessee, January, 1993.

7. James W. Kuhn and Donald W. Shriver, Jr., *Beyond Success: Corporations and Their Critics in the 1990s* (New York: Oxford Univ. Press, 1991), 301.

8. Parker J. Palmer, "Divided No More: A Movement Approach to Educational Reform," *Change* 24 (March-April 1992): 10–17.

9. Parker Palmer, recounted at workshop, Nashville, Tennessee, January 1993.

10. James Gustafson, *Ethics from a Theocentric Perspective,* vol. 1, *Theology and Ethics* (Chicago: Univ. of Chicago Press, 1981), 224, 232.

11. Gustafson describes the components of moral discernment in *Ethics from a Theocentric Perspective,* 333–42; quote is from p. 338.

11. Making the Appropriate Response

1. Mary Field Belenky, et al., *Women's Ways of Knowing: The Development of Self, Voice, and Mind* (New York: Basic Books, 1986), 167.

2. Lisa Sowle Cahill, "Can Theology Have a Role in 'Public' Bioethical Discourse?" in "Theology, Religious Traditions and Bioethics," ed. by Daniel Callahan and Courtney S. Campbell. Special Supplement, *Hastings Center Report,* 20 (July-August 1990), 12.

3. Kathy E. Ferguson, *The Feminist Case Against Bureaucracy* (Philadelphia: Temple Univ. Press, 1984), 198. My sense of the discussions that are structured by agendas is captured in Ferguson's description of the "the cooperative and respectful processes of talking and listening that express care and maintain connection."

4. MacIntyre, *After Virtue,* especially chapter 1.

5. Bruce Jennings, "Bioethics as Civic Discourse," *Hastings Center Report* 19 (September-October 1989): 35.

6. Martin Luther King, Jr., *Stride Toward Freedom* (New York: Harper and Bros., 1958), 213.

7. Weisband and Franck, *Resignation in Protest,* 12.

8. Gary Trudeau, *Doonesbury,* Universal Press Syndicate.

9. Martin Luther, Speech at the Diet of Worms, April 18, 1521.

Conclusion: Agendas and Personal Integrity

1. Kekes, "Self-direction," 14; on conscience, Little, "Duties of Station vs. Duties of Conscience," 147; on integrity, Walzer, *Obligations,* 196; on judgment, Postema, "Moral Responsibility in Professional Ethics," 68.

Select Bibliography

Anderson, Robert, et al. *Divided Loyalties.* West Lafayette, Ind.: Purdue Univ. Press, 1980.

Bateson, Mary Catherine. *Composing a Life.* New York: Atlantic Monthly Press, 1989.

Bayles, Michael. *Professional Ethics.* Belmont, Calif.: Wadsworth Publishing Co., 1981.

Belenky, Mary Field, et al. *Women's Ways of Knowing: The Development of Self, Voice, and Mind.* New York: Basic Books, 1986.

Bellah, Robert N., William M. Sullivan, Ann Swidler, and Steven M. Tipton. *The Good Society.* New York: Alfred A. Knopf, 1991.

Bellah, Robert N., Richard Madsen, William M. Sullivan, Ann Swidler, and Steven M. Tipton. *Habits of the Heart: Individualism and Commitment in American Life.* Berkeley: Univ. of California Press, 1985.

Berger, Peter L., and Thomas Luckmann. *The Social Construction of Reality.* Garden City, N.Y.: Doubleday and Co., 1966.

Bok, Sissela. *Lying: Moral Choice in Public and Private Life.* New York: Random House, 1979.

——. "Whistleblowing and Professional Responsibilities." In *Ethics Teaching in Higher Education,* ed. Daniel Callahan and Sissela Bok, 277–95. New York: Plenum Press, 1980.

Bowie, Norman. "'Role' as a Moral Concept in Health Care." *Journal of Medicine and Philosophy* 7, no. 1 (1982): 57–63.

Bowman, James S., Frederick A. Elliston, and Paul Lockhart. *Professional Dissent: An Annotated Bibliography and Resource Guide.* New York: Garfield, 1984.

Burden, Jonathan, and Terry M. Moe. "Agenda Control, Committee Capture and the Dynamics of Institutional Politics." *American Political Science Review* 80 (December 1986): 1187–1207.

Cahill, Lisa Sowle. "Can Theology Have a Role in 'Public' Bioethical Discourse?" in "Theology, Religious Tradition and Bioethics," ed. by

Daniel Callahan and Courtney S. Campbell. Special Supplement, *Hastings Center Report*, 20 (July-August 1990): 10–14.

Callahan, Sidney. *In Good Conscience: Reason and Emotion in Moral Decision Making.* San Francisco: Harper San Francisco, 1991.

Camenisch, Paul F. *Grounding Professional Ethics in a Pluralistic Society.* New York: Haven, 1983.

Carr, Albert Z. "Can an Executive Afford a Conscience?" *Harvard Business Review* 48 (July-August 1970): 58–64.

_____. "Is Business Bluffing Ethical?" *Harvard Business Review* 46 (January-February 1968): 143–53.

Cobb, Roger W., and Charles D. Elder. *Participation in American Politics: The Dynamics of Agenda Building.* 2d ed. Baltimore: Johns Hopkins Univ. Press, 1983.

Cobb, Roger, Jennie-Keith Ross, and Marc Howard Ross. "Agenda Building as a Comparative Political Process." *American Political Science Review* 70 (March 1976): 126–38.

Davis, Michael. "Avoiding the Tragedy of Whistleblowing." *Business and Professional Ethics Journal* 8 (Winter 1989): 3–19.

_____. "Thinking Like an Engineer: The Place of a Code of Ethics in the Practice of a Profession." *Philosophy and Public Affairs* 20, no. 2 (1991): 150–67.

DeGeorge, Richard T. "Ethical Responsibilities of Engineers in Large Corporations: The Pinto Case." *Business and Professional Ethics Journal* 2, no. 1 (1982): 15–25.

Dobel, J. Patrick. *Compromise and Political Action: Political Morality in Liberal and Democratic Life.* Savage, Md.: Rowman and Littlefield Publishers, 1990.

Downie, R. S. "Responsibility and Social Roles." In *Individual and Collective Responsibility,* ed. Peter A. French, 65–80. Cambridge, Mass.: Schenkman, 1972.

Ebaugh, Helen Rose Fuchs. *Becoming an Ex: The Process of Role Exit.* Chicago: Univ. of Chicago Press, 1988.

Elliston, Frederick A., John Keenan, Paul Lockhart, and Jane van Schiask. *Whistleblowing: Managing Dissent in the Workplace.* New York: Praeger, 1985.

Emmet, Dorothy. *Rules, Roles, and Relations.* New York: St. Martin's, 1966.

Etzioni, Amitai. *The Semi-Professions and Their Organization.* New York: The Council, 1979.

_____, ed. *The Moral Dimension: Toward a New Economics.* New York: The Free Press, 1988.

Ewing, David. *Freedom Inside the Organization.* New York: McGraw-Hill, 1977.

Ferguson, Kathy E. *The Feminist Case Against Bureaucracy.* Philadelphia: Temple Univ. Press, 1984.

Fleishman, Joel, and Bruce Payne. *Ethical Dilemmas and the Education of Policy Makers.* Hastings-on-Hudson, N.Y.: Hastings Center, 1980.

Fletcher, Joseph. *Situation Ethics: The New Morality.* Philadelphia: Westminster Press, 1966.

Flores, Albert, and Deborah G. Johnson. "Collective Responsibility and Professional Roles." *Ethics* 93, no. 3 (1983): 537–45.

Frankena, William. *Ethics.* 2d ed. Englewood Cliffs, N.J.: Prentice-Hall, 1973.

Freedman, Benjamin. "A Meta-Ethics for Professional Morality." *Ethics* 89 (1978): 1–19.

――――. "What Really Makes Professional Morality Different: Response to Martin." *Ethics* 91, no. 4 (1981): 626–30.

Fritzsch, David J. "A Model of Decision-Making Incorporating Ethical Values." *Journal of Business Ethics* 10 (November 1991): 841–52.

Gewirth, Alan. "Professional Ethics: The Separatist Thesis." *Ethics* 96, no. 2 (1986): 282–300.

Gibbard, Allan. "Communities of Judgment." *Social Philosophy and Policy* 7, no. 1 (1989): 175–89.

Giddens, Anthony. *The Consequences of Modernity.* Stanford, Calif.: Stanford Univ. Press, 1990.

Gilligan, Carol. *In a Different Voice: Psychological Theory and Women's Development.* Cambridge, Mass.: Harvard Univ. Press, 1982.

Gilligan, Carol, et al., eds. *Mapping the Moral Domain: A Contribution of Women's Thinking to Psychology and Education.* Cambridge, Mass.: Harvard Univ. Press, 1988.

Glazer, Myron Peretz, and Penina Migdal Glazer. "Individual Ethics and Organizational Morality." In *Ethics, Government and Public Policy: A Reference Guide,* ed. James S. Bowman and Frederick A. Elliston, 55–78. New York: Greenwood Press, 1988.

Goldman, Alan H. *The Moral Foundations of Professional Ethics.* Totowa, N.J.: Rowman and Littlefield, 1980.

Goode, William J. "Community within a Community." *American Sociological Review* 22 (1957): 194–200.

Gustafson, James. *Ethics from a Theocentric Perspective.* Vol. I, *Theology and Ethics.* Chicago: Univ. of Chicago Press, 1981.

Gutmann, Amy, and Dennis Thompson, eds. *Ethics and Politics: Cases and Comments.* 2d ed. Chicago: Nelson-Hall Publishers, 1990.

Hampshire, Stuart. *Public and Private Morality.* Cambridge, N.Y.: Cambridge Univ. Press, 1978.

Heineman, Robert A., William T. Bluhm, Steven A. Peterson, and Edward N.

Kearny. *The World of the Policy Analyst: Rationality, Values, and Politics.* Chatham, N.J.: Chatham House Publishers, 1990.

Hirschman, Albert O. *Exit, Voice and Loyalty: Responses to Declines in Firms, Organizations and States.* Cambridge, Mass.: Harvard Univ. Press, 1970.

Hofeller, Kathleen H. *Social, Psychological and Situational Factors in Wife Abuse.* Palo Alto, Calif.: R and E Research Associates, 1982.

Howard, W. Kenneth. "Must Public Hands Be Dirty?" *Journal of Value Inquiry* 11, no. 1 (1977): 29–40.

Jack, Rand, and Dana Crowley Jack. *Moral Vision and Professional Decisions: The Changing Values of Women and Men Lawyers.* New York: Cambridge Univ. Press, 1989.

Jennings, Bruce. "Bioethics as Civic Discourse." *Hastings Center Report* 19 (September-October 1989): 34–35.

Jennings, Bruce, Daniel Callahan, and Susan M. Wolf. "The Professions: Public Interest and Common Good." In "The Public Duties of the Professions," Special Supplement, *The Hastings Center Report* 17, no. 1 (1987): 3–10.

Jones, W. T. "Public Roles, Private Roles, and Differential Assessments of Role Performance." *Ethics* 94, no. 4 (1984): 602–20.

Jonsen, Albert R., and Stephen Toulmin. *The Abuse of Casuistry: A History of Moral Reasoning.* Berkeley: Univ. of California Press, 1988.

King, Martin Luther, Jr. *Stride Toward Freedom.* New York: Harper and Bros., 1958.

———. *Why We Can't Wait.* New York: Harper and Row, 1963.

Kingdom, John W. *Agendas, Alternatives and Public Policies.* Boston: Little Brown and Co., 1984.

Kolenda, Konstantin, ed. *Organizations and Ethical Individualism.* New York: Greenwood-Praeger, 1988.

Kuhn, James W., and Donald W. Shriver, Jr. *Beyond Success: Corporations and Their Critics in the 1990s.* New York: Oxford Univ. Press, 1991.

Lachs, John. "'I Only Work Here': Mediation and Irresponsibility." In *Ethics, Free Enterprise, and Public Policy,* ed. Richard T. DeGeorge and Joseph A. Pilcher, 201–13. New York: Oxford Univ. Press, 1978.

Ladd, John. "Morality and the Ideal of Rationality in Formal Organization." *Monist* 54 (1970): 488–516.

Paul Leinberger, and Bruce Tucker. *The New Individualists: The Generation after the Organization Man.* New York: Harper Collins, 1991.

Little, David. "Duties of Station vs. Duties of Conscience: Are There Two Moralities?" In *Private and Public Ethics: Tensions Between Conscience and Institutional Responsibility,* ed. Donald G. Jones, 125–57. New York: Edwin Mellen Press, 1978.

MacIntyre, Alasdair. *After Virtue.* 2d ed. Notre Dame, Ind.: Univ. of Notre Dame Press, 1984.

March, James, and Johan P. Olsen, "The New Institutionalism: Organizational Factors in Political Life." *American Political Science Review* 78 (September 1984): 734–49.

Martin, Mike W. "Professional and Ordinary Morality: A Reply to Freedman." *Ethics* 91, no. 4 (1981): 631–33.

————. "Rights and the Meta-Ethics of Professional Morality." *Ethics* 91, no. 4 (1981): 619–25.

McDonald, Ross A., and Bart Victor. "Towards the Integration of the Individual and Moral Agencies." *Business and Professional Ethics Journal* 7 (Fall-Winter 1988): 103–18.

McDowell, Banks. *Ethical Conduct and the Professional's Dilemma: Choosing Between Service and Success.* New York: Quorum Books, 1991.

Merton, Robert. *Social Theory and Social Structure.* 3d ed. New York: The Free Press, 1968.

Mount, Eric. *Professional Ethics in Context: Institutions, Images and Empathy.* Louisville, Ky.: Westminster/John Knox Press, 1990.

Niebuhr, H. Richard. *The Responsible Self: An Essay in Christian Moral Philosophy.* New York: Harper and Row, 1963.

Norton, David L. *Personal Destinies.* Princeton: Princeton Univ. Press, 1976.

Oldenquist, Andrew. "Loyalties." *The Journal of Philosophy* 79 (April 1982): 173–93.

Pincoffs, Edmond L. *Quandaries and Virtues.* Lawrence: Univ. of Kansas Press, 1986.

Postema, Gerald J. "Moral Responsibility in Professional Ethics." *New York University Law Review* 55 (April 1980): 63–89.

Robison, Wade L., Michael S. Pritchard, and Joseph Ellin, eds. *Profits and Professions: Essays in Business and Professional Ethics.* Clifton, N.J.: Humana Press, 1983.

Rohr, John. *Ethics for Bureaucrats.* New York: Dekker, 1978.

Ross, Maggie, *Pillars of Flame: Power, Priesthood, and Spiritual Maturity.* San Francisco: Harper and Row, 1988.

————. *The Fire of Your Life.* New York: Paulist Press, 1983.

Salisbury, Robert. "Interest Representation: The Dominance of Institutions." *American Political Science Review* 78 (March 1984): 64–76.

Scott, William G., and David K. Hart. *Organizational Values in America.* New Brunswick, N.J.: Transaction Publishers, 1989.

Sheehy, Gail. *Passages: Predictable Crises of Adult Life.* New York: E. P. Dutton and Co., 1976.

Smith, Rogers. "Political Jurisprudence, the 'New Institutionalism,' and the Future of Public Law." *American Political Science Review* 82 (March 1988): 89–108.

Snoeyenbos, Milton, Robert Aldemar, and James Humber, eds. *Business Ethics: Corporate Values and Society.* Buffalo, N.Y.: Prometheus Books, 1983.

Stout, Jeffrey. *Ethics after Babel: The Language of Morals and Their Discontents.* Boston: Beacon Press, 1988.

Thoreau, Henry David. *The Portable Thoreau,* ed. Carol Bode. New York: The Viking Press, 1947.

Thompson, Dennis F. *Political Ethics and Public Office.* Cambridge, Mass.: Harvard Univ. Press, 1987.

Urmson, J. O. "Saints and Heroes." In *Essays in Moral Philosophy,* ed. A. I. Melden, 198–216. Seattle: Univ. of Washington Press, 1958.

Walker, Lenore E. *The Battered Woman.* New York: Harper & Row, 1970.

_____. *The Battered Woman Syndrome.* New York: Springer Publishing Co., 1984.

Walsh, W. H. "Pride, Shame and Responsibility." *Philosophical Quarterly* 20 (January 1970): 1–13.

Walzer, Michael. "Political Action: The Problem of Dirty Hands." *Philosophy and Public Affairs* 2, no. 2 (1973): 160–80.

_____. *Obligations: Essays on Disobedience, War, and Citizenship.* Cambridge, Mass.: Harvard Univ. Press, 1970.

Wartenberg, Thomas E. "Teaching Women Philosophy." *Teaching Philosophy* 11, no. 1 (1988): 15–24.

Weber, Max. "Politics as a Vocation." In *From Max Weber,* trans. and ed. H. H. Gerth and C. Wright Mills, 77–128. New York: Oxford Univ. Press, 1958.

Weisband, Edward, and Thomas M. Franck. *Resignation in Protest: Political and Ethical Choices between Loyalty to Team and Loyalty to Conscience in American Public Life.* New York: Grossman Publishers, 1975.

Westin, Alan. *Whistle Blowing!* New York: McGraw-Hill, 1981.

Wilensky, Harold L. "The Professionalization of Everyone?" *American Journal of Sociology* 70 (1964): 137–58.

Index